Children Don't Come with a Manual

A Guidebook on How to Discipline with Love

12-21-24

Every child is a
Unique masterpiece.

Marikit Villasis - Corbin

Marikit Villasis - Corbin

outskirts
press

The opinions expressed in this manuscript are solely the opinions of the author and do not represent the opinions or thoughts of the publisher. The author has represented and warranted full ownership and/or legal right to publish all the materials in this book.

Children Don't Come with a Manual
A Guidebook on How to Discipline with Love
All Rights Reserved.
Copyright © 2016 Marikit Villasis - Corbin
v4.0

Cover Photo © 2016 Marikit Villasis. All rights reserved - used with permission.

This book may not be reproduced, transmitted, or stored in whole or in part by any means, including graphic, electronic, or mechanical without the express written consent of the publisher except in the case of brief quotations embodied in critical articles and reviews.

Outskirts Press, Inc.
http://www.outskirtspress.com

ISBN: 978-1-4787-7545-4

Outskirts Press and the "OP" logo are trademarks belonging to Outskirts Press, Inc.

PRINTED IN THE UNITED STATES OF AMERICA

For my children, the loves of my life: Paulina, Jethro, Stephanie and Hermès.

For my sister, Marilag, and brothers, Maharlika, Matagumpay and Maharlakan.

I love you all with all my heart.

My loyal and beloved dogs, Polo and Brucie. May you rest in peace.

For my companion the last eight years through thick and thin – Coco Banana... ☺

My partner and loving husband, Ken.

Table of Contents

PREFACE vii
INTRODUCTION ix
1 RAPPORT: An Emotional Foundation 1
2 THE PARENT AS THE PARENT 6
3 HANDLING UNDESIRABLE BEHAVIOR 11
4 THE POSITIVE REWARD SYSTEM 16
5 THE CONTRACT 23
6 TIME-OUT, REVERSE TIME-OUT, AND PHYSICAL RESTRAINT 29
7 ENVIRONMENTAL CONTROL 38
8 TO SPANK OR NOT TO SPANK, THAT IS THE QUESTION 41
9 THE FEEDBACK TECHNIQUE 46
10 THE MUTUAL PROBLEM-SOLVING TECHNIQUE 53

11	THE FAMILY COUNCIL..................................59
12	PARENTAL MUSCLE 64
13	TEACHING OUR CHILDREN ETHICS AND MORALITY..70
14	THE ART OF NEGATIVE THINKING AND DESENSITIZATION..76
15	STEPPARENTING AND THE BLENDED FAMILY 81
16	RIGHTS OF THE CHILD – SUMMARY.............88
17	THE RIGHTS OF THE PARENTS....................101
18	DEVELOPMENTAL STAGES...........................108
About the Author: 123	

PREFACE

Whenever we acquire or purchase something, more often than not, it comes with a manual. When we buy a television set, it has a manual. When we buy food, a toy, a new dress, it always has some form of instruction on how to handle it. But when we had our children, where was the manual??? Was there a kit that told us how to handle it? There was no instruction guide whatsoever that tells us what to do when the baby starts crying. It is always a what if. If they cry a certain way, they could be this or that, so try this and that.

Fact is: When you go to a pet shop, the sales clerk gives you guidelines on how to feed and bathe your new pet, together with all the other dos and don'ts as it grows up. I know, it's pretty much the same when we have a child. The most we get the very minute the baby pops out are tons of information on how other people raised their children. From the traditional to the bizarre, I'm sure you've heard them all.

Many books have now been written on how to discipline a

child. We all know too well that there is no foolproof way to bring up a child into this world. If anyone out there had absolutely no problem raising their children, I sure would like to read your book.

More often than not, parents realize too late the mistakes they've made in bringing up their children. This thoughtful and simple–to-understand guide provides various options for proper discipline at the right moment and at the right age of the child in the manner that is called for.

In this day and age when parents are more conscious to become better parents and individuals for their children, the concept of children as "better seen than heard" no longer applies to most of us. Though my siblings and I were raised in this manner, and all turned out to be good and productive individuals, it does have its pros and cons.
I'm sure we would all agree that we want our children to experience a joyful and rich childhood development as much as we want to enjoy parenthood in the best possible way we can.

So allow me to share some scientific studies in layman's terms. Parenting isn't rocket science but neither is it a walk in the park.

Enjoy your reading and here's hoping that I am able to assist you in some way.

INTRODUCTION

Countless books, pamphlets, and articles have been written about child discipline. Schools have also participated in molding our children into better individuals. They send out pamphlets and reading materials to help us provide a systematic structure in guiding our children to become successful adults.

Let us begin by defining what discipline is. Mr. Webster says: It is the systematic and rigorous training of the mental, moral and physical powers by instruction and exercise. The result then is – obedience.

So, if we take into context Mr. Webster's definition, key words would be: systematic, training, instruction, and exercise. Simply put, *discipline is teaching by the adult and learning for the child.*

Discipline is thereby a process of teaching that goes on all the time. However, we should bear in mind that <u>no one approach will work with all the children at all times.</u> Different approaches are applied to each and every child and in each and every situation. This is precisely why we call our children unique individuals.

The age of the child should always be taken into account. I found it extremely strange that most theories of discipline I came across seldom mention about age consideration. Obviously, we do not specify desirable behavior the same way we would a two-year-old, an eight-year-old, or a fifteen-year-old. There is also the factor of foundation. A child may only be eight, but because he or she is exposed to adults all the time, the child's thinking and behavior is not like that of a typical eight-year-old. There are many factors that need to be considered when attempting to apply a method of teaching.

There are also many theories that do not make allowance for differences in parents. When we discipline our children, we have to take into account whether the particular method we want to apply would be comfortable for the parent. We cannot ask a parent to spank a child if it is not in their nature or culture to inflict harm, no matter what the degree or severity of the undesirable behavior is.

Although numerous psychological studies recommend that a particular approach works best in specific situations, it may work for parent A but not necessarily for parent B, parent C, or D, E, F.

Because of these reasons, I believe that we should provide new and more flexible approaches to discipline. It is then my goal to be able to provide other parents with these commonsensical yet invaluable tools.

My principle for this book is that: No specific approach is applicable to all children. It's as simple as that. If there is more than one way to skin a cat, then there should be more than one way to teach a child. Makes sense right?

If some children are easier or harder to mold or handle than other children, this may be attributed to their innate biological temperament. Genetics play an important role. Remember that each parent contributes 23 chromosomes to their child. Remember when your mother would say, "You take after your father so much!" when she was upset or disappointed with you? (Although this may not necessarily be true.)

Another important factor is the child's age. There are formative years to consider as well as most psychologists would refer to. It would be difficult to retrain a child, or even an adult for that matter, if their character and personality had been set. It may be altered, modified, relearned, or reintroduced with specific methods and programs which may or may not prove to provide significant improvements. Given this reason, we recommend teaching a child at the earliest time possible. And yes, even as early as the moment they come out of the womb. We need to find the right combination of methods to be able to teach the child desirable behavior.

Since this book takes into consideration various aspects of the child as a unique individual, we take on a developmental approach from birth until the child becomes an adult. Bear in mind that this material is a combination of personal experiences, theories, research, experimentation, and learnings from experienced individuals. I do not claim to be an expert. But I am considered a specialist.

After the strategies are presented, I shall take you through the development of a hypothetical child from birth to age 21. Once you have familiarized yourself with the teaching strategies and attempt to apply them, remember that like any new method, it is bound to make you feel strange, most especially if you have been used to a single technique, or not aware of any at all. However, if you find that after sincere efforts, the recommended method still makes you feel strange, remember that it's not you. Do not hesitate to drop it and try another technique.

Discipline is something that goes on all the time. We may not even be aware of it but even when we think we do not interact with our children, they continuously learn from our behavior and their environment. They observe us all the time. As a matter of fact, one of the techniques I use during training or clinical assessment is to allow the participants or subjects to observe me first. I call it breaking the ice silently.

I walk around the room to prepare my materials and familiarize myself with the surroundings. It allows me to be comfortable and at the same time gives the participants the needed time to size me up. Which is okay, because considering the fact that I am about to introduce something new or different, this process is necessary.

THE ART OF TEACHING IS THE ART OF ASSISTING DISCOVERY.

Mark Van Doren

1
RAPPORT: An Emotional Foundation

Since discipline is really teaching, we can just imagine from thousands of experiments that we can practically teach anyone or anything to learn a particular behavior. Not only can we teach nonverbalized infants sign language to swimming, but we can also teach dogs, elephants, birds, hamsters, and dolphins—almost any animal we can name. Trust me, whether we are taking any action or not, we are always teaching someone something. So why not put in the effort to let them learn positive behavior?

We may not realize it, but teaching animals is similar to

teaching humans. (Well, sometimes animals are easier to teach!) Of course, what sets them apart is that humans are more "human" and we have a higher intelligence than other animals. That's precisely why whenever I come across individuals who do not think before they speak, my thought bubble goes haywire, trying to figure out why they are thinking like…an animal.

Therefore, how do we teach desirable behavior? Commonly, and as what is socially acceptable, we refer to desirable behavior such as not hitting other children when at play, obeying parents' reasonable requests, and cooperating in school; while undesirable behavior means otherwise. The exact opposite of what we ask them to do or basically anything that makes parents go ballistic and say: "What were you thinking???" or, "What were you *not* thinking???"

One thing to remember is that when we would like to teach our children something or make things work out in our normal day-to-day lives, we oftentimes need to establish an emotional foundation to be able to relay whatever message we would like to convey. It is always important that we establish good rapport whenever we have intentions of establishing any form of relationship. This applies to work or any form of leadership or team environment we are in. We adults could fully understand that. And of course, credibility plays an important role. Your child may obey you only because he doesn't want to hurt your feelings. But wouldn't you want to teach your child positive behavior because you are their role model?

RAPPORT: AN EMOTIONAL FOUNDATION

In our daily lives, we encounter people like doctors who establish rapport with their patients to gain their trust and confidence, and the same with priests, teachers, salesmen, lawyers, almost any job one can imagine that involves interaction. Come to think of it, as uncanny as it may seem, we also establish some form of rapport with non-living things. Most people take the time first to "get to know" their new phone, laptop, Kitchen-Aid, or anything techy or electronic. If we can take the time to get to know things, doesn't it make more sense to get to know people first?

It is essential to establish rapport. By rapport, we mean a mutual liking and respect and good vibes between both parties. A simple concept most of us sometimes overlook.

Can you just imagine if the word *rapport* was not at all conceived? There would be more invasion of one's territory, disrespect, and inconsideration, resulting in more hurt feelings in this world than it already has. The workplace is a perfect example. If you are a new manager and you immediately start ordering people around, acting like a BOSS, you are bound to fail. A true manager and leader would know better how to handle this situation.

I remember my first time as a volunteer psychologist at the Department of Social Welfare. My subjects were abused children. Thereby making them "extra special" participants. It was not easy helping them recover from their experience with the cruelties of life at an early age. Most of them were withdrawn and incredulous. My first task was always to establish rapport by letting them "check me out" first. I pretend to arrange the toys, walking back and forth around the room as they watch. I then ask silly questions such as: Do you think it's going to rain today? What time is it? or Do you want a donut? (Which I always make sure I bring).

This provides room for the child to feel that they are not objects being moved around or studied. It gives them enough time to absorb what is happening in their surroundings. And more often than not, since children have the purest of hearts, they will be able to judge our actions as something for their own good. Whether they are children with special needs or children who are labelled "normal" by our society, rapport should always be established.

Since children take approximately a year to outgrow the infant stage and begin to crawl or walk, problems with discipline do not usually arise until they are toddlers. This means we have one solid year and another to establish rapport with our baby. All this time that we took care of them, bathed them, fed them, sang to them, in their eyes, they are very much loved. And all they want to do is to please us. As they become toddlers, we begin to teach them how to and how not to behave in certain ways, and we then have a huge deposit of rapport to draw upon. I call it the love bank: the more deposits you make, the more you can save up in times of need. Forgiveness, for example. As an adult, it is easier to forgive someone who has done more positive things than bad.

Rapport is a continuous building process. We must be conscious so as not to end up being a "command-giver" or in

RAPPORT: AN EMOTIONAL FOUNDATION

most cases, an emotional blackmailer, where we either end up giving orders all the time without considering the other choices the child may have, or we are always threatening to feel bad if the child does not obey our request.

Spending time with our children should simply be an enjoyable experience and not a task. Of course, the things we do together with our children should vary depending on their age and their stage of development. A senior psychiatrist friend of mine once told me that generation gaps are the result of parents not taking the time to find rapport-building activities for them and their teenagers. However, those who do have a smoother flow of relationship with them.

Famous words from John Masefield, a poet: *"The days that makes us happy, make us wise."* And I shall add that the wiser we become, the better individuals we shall be. The better individuals we become, the better place this world will be.

2
The Parent As the Parent

I have read way too many materials lamenting the decline of firm parental discipline and the rise of parents' permissiveness. In most cases, being too patient and giving in to your children results in disrespect and taking parents for granted. Though this must not be misconstrued as having a relationship with your children like friends is unacceptable. What this chapter aims to tell you is that whatever style of relationship you decide to have with your children, it is of utmost importance that we establish our authority as parents.

However, there are also materials that recommend permissiveness as a parenting style. But before we move on, what is permissiveness anyway? By being permissive, parents are afraid to say no to their children. They are afraid to set limits, and in general have abdicated their authority as a parent

THE PARENT AS THE PARENT

and have turned it over to their children. This is the scenario where children basically rule the household. When your life is governed by a single child and your world basically revolves around that child, you have a serious problem. And by serious, I mean, you are doomed.

Let me define permissiveness in this manner by citing an example in the Asian culture, the Filipino culture to be precise. I have reason to believe that in the Filipino culture (which we have acquired from the Spaniards, Americans, and Chinese), the majority of Filipino parents are **not** permissive. We run our families; **we do not** abdicate our authority. We are matriarchal in nature. Most of us, even relatives to the nth degree of consanguinity, consult with the elders before making decisions. This we may attribute to the huge percentage of children raised in this manner who do not get into trouble with the law and do not cause problems in school. Again, like any systematic method, it has its pros and cons. But I must say, this type of culture presents more advantages.

This chapter is not addressed to parents who have retained their family authority but to the minority who are desperately trying to keep control over their children and not succeeding. If you are a parent whose child refuses to obey *reasonable* parental authority, then you have a real problem. Because every discipline technique, method, or style should have the groundwork of a child's basic willingness to obey parental authority.

Whether a child is a toddler, a preschooler, or a teenager, if they know that they have the power in the family, then we have already lost a parent. This is no different from a boss whose employees pay no attention to whatever he says. He continues to come to the office like a figurehead that does not possess any leadership.

There are two causes of parental permissiveness. First, many parents are uncertain and apprehensive on how to bring up their children. In the old pre-child-psychology days, parents were not aware that the way they raised their children would determine how they would turn out as adults. They simply had no idea if their children would turn out to be future presidents of the country or the next drug lord.

When I was younger, I would often hear the word "disposition" from adults. They used this to describe their children or other people's children. They referred to one child as having a happy disposition, the other with a sunny disposition, the other with a good disposition, and if the child was behaving badly and fighting with other children, they would say he has a mean disposition. As I got older, I then understood what they meant.

By disposition, we refer to the innate temperament and personality of the child, which would then emerge in later childhood and in adult life. Without the learning of modern psychology, this was how our parents gauged what would become of us in the future. Although this theory may still apply in some form, we only consider it as one of the many factors of why a person is the way they are.

THE PARENT AS THE PARENT

Although an important effect of our knowledge on sophisticated psychology is important, many of us are unsure whether our way of raising our children is the correct manner. Bear in mind though that as much as our great-grandparents were not conscious of their ways in raising their children, they took firm and decisive action, based on common sense.

In today's modern world, and after countless studies conducted by scientists, psychologists, and doctors, coupled with data from the experienced adults and the elderly, child psychology, or even adult psychology, tells us that age, stage of development, and inherited characteristics of an individual are key elements to determine which type of discipline technique would be suitable to a particular child. We need to know how to teach or discipline our child at each stage in their life. Every parent needs to have a basic knowledge of child psychology or teaching, because every parent, whether they are aware of it or not, is a child psychologist and a teacher.

Now, the next (and major) cause of parental permissiveness: When a parent constantly appeases a child and gives in to their whims and demands, allowing the child to push them around, the parent is doing so because of a basic psychological reason: compensation. Some of you might find this reasoning absurd, but this is an unconscious motto, especially for single/separated parents or parents who work in far places or whose jobs often take their time away from their family. We need to accept and realize that relationships with our children differ from others. There is no perfect scenario. Of course you have to work. And sometimes relationships with our partners don't work out the way we want them to.

Remember: the situation that we put our children in is always based on the judgments we make. No child is in any situation they are in because of their own choice. The best we can do as adults is to make prudent decisions. And yes, this includes who the other parent of YOUR child will be, whether biological or blended (step family). This way, no parent would have to compensate and end up being permissive. Because at the end of the day, having a permissive parent disables a child's opportunity to be the best person they can be as an adult.

3
HANDLING UNDESIRABLE BEHAVIOR

In the earlier chapters, we learned how to build desirable behavior. In this chapter, we will learn how to handle bad behavior.

In my early years as a parent, I've heard numerous concerns, from a child biting another child, to a mother whose seven-year-old son is beating up smaller children or their eleven-year-old stealing from stores.

Before we learn how to deal with undesirable behavior, let us discuss how not to. Most of us parents try to deal with undesirable behavior with punishment power. It is important, therefore, to make sure you know why punishment power is a very poor and inefficient method, and often ends up making the undesirable behavior worse rather than better. When parents use punishment, they scold, yell, lecture (or, as my kids call it, *sermon*) take away privileges, threaten, or even spank.

What is wrong with these kinds of punishments? Let me enumerate:

1. This violates the law of the soggy potato chip theory that we will discuss later on.
2. A person who punishes is teaching other people to avoid him. How can you be an important and positive influence in your child's life when he wants to avoid you because you are a scolder, moralizer, yeller, or spanker?
3. Punishment is merely an attempt to curb undesirable behavior. Punishment in itself does not teach or motivate a child towards more desirable behavior. Punishment tells a child <u>what not to do</u>; it does not tell him <u>what to do</u>. Then again, if punishment works as a system of teaching people good behavior, then why is it that when criminals are released from jail, they are supposed to lead straight lives as law-abiding citizens. But guess what? Studies have shown otherwise (according to a report published on the Telegraph, a UK paper. A study showed that 74 percent of criminals commit at least one crime within nine years after being released). It has been learned that a high percentage of those released have gone back to prison in a relatively short pe-

riod of time. Why then do you think our justice system keeps on increasing the number of years of a criminal's stay in prison? Perhaps because when they are released, they would be too old to commit any crime! Or so we hope.

4. Punishment loses its effectiveness as children grow older. Punishment power may be temporarily effective for children ages five to seven. But when a child reaches the age of eleven or twelve or into their teens, the old devices of taking away privileges or scolding or spanking have lost their effectiveness.

Since most of us grew up not being exposed to other forms of discipline or ways to handle misbehavior, we are only knowledgeable to the idea that punishment is the only way to deal with undesirable behavior. Let's analyze these methods of punishment if they were used on adults:

<u>Scolding</u> - I was once watching a television show wherein a husband came home late from "work" and the wife had been waiting all night long on the couch. When the husband opened the door, trying not to make any sound, the wife suddenly stood up from the couch and said, "Where did you come from again? You didn't even bother to call! I was waiting for you all evening! I tried to call you but your mobile was off! Don't tell me its low battery again! How many times have we agreed that whenever you think you will be late, at least have the decency to call? How would I know that? I can't possibly imagine that there was no land phone at all where you came from!" Blah, blah, blah and so

on and on and on...

Analyze this kind of scolding. It's similar to the things that parents say to children. Would you like to be on the receiving end of this criticism? Does it motivate you to change your behavior in the future? I think not! As a matter of fact, as we get older, scolding mutates into a different name: nagging.

Lecturing – You accidently hit your husband's new car as you backed your car out of the garage. He lectures you. "Honey, how many times did I tell you, every time you back out of the garage, you have to ask for assistance because it would be difficult for you to see any incoming vehicle from both sides. You don't back up looking just at the mirror. That's precisely the reason why I don't want you to back it up by yourself. I think I'll have to treat you like a ten-month-old child because that's exactly how you are behaving. I don't understand you at all!"

How do you like the lecture? Does it motivate you to be more careful next time? I think not! I'm sure it would probably make you feel like deliberately backing up into his car all over again! Once again, many children are unwilling listeners to such lectures from their parents.

Taking away privileges – Let's say you have overspent the family budget for food and household expenses for this month. It is only the eighteenth of the month and you still have up to the end of the month to supply your family with food but you have no more money left. Then your husband

HANDLING UNDESIRABLE BEHAVIOR

tells you he is sorry but he will have to take away your budget for trips to the spa and salon for the next six months! How does that make you feel? Does that motivate you to do a better job at budgeting family expense? I think not! I'm sure it will make you furious and feel like overspending again next month's budget!

<u>Spanking</u> – Again, you are not able to keep your checkbook balanced, and consequently, you find that you are five hundred dollars short due to a check that you just wrote for the children's school bus. Since checks are bouncing left and right, your husband grabs you, takes you into the bedroom, and hits you hard with his belt. Does this make you extra careful with the budget next time? Or does it make you furious at your husband and determined to get back at him in some way?

We can obviously see the absurdity of trying to compel adults to more desirable behavior by inflicting punishment. But somehow, we have difficulty seeing that it is just as absurd to expect punishment to teach desirable behavior to children.

Punishment power produces hostility, resentment, and the desire for retaliation in children, teenagers, and adults.
So, if punishment is a poor and inefficient way of dealing with undesirable behavior, what can we use in its place? Read on as we tackle alternatives to punishment in dealing with misbehavior.

4
THE POSITIVE REWARD SYSTEM

The most common discipline strategy most of us implement but are not aware of is the positive reward system. This may be likened to Pavlov's reward and reinforcement theory. Unfortunately, studies have shown that although this is one of the most common discipline methods, it is more often than not used the opposite way.

Let me give you an example based on animal behavior. My beloved dog was a half-breed German pointer. He supposedly came from a breed of disciplined and loyal dogs, but because he was not purebred, he was temperamental and difficult to teach. With much patience and love, we were able to teach him to sit down, shake hands, and be still when

THE POSITIVE REWARD SYSTEM

asked to. We didn't have to resort to screaming and yelling or lectures (well, once in a while), nor was he spanked in any way. Not at all. As a matter of fact, he became one of the most loyal four-legged friends anyone could ever have. He waited for us to come home and yes, he knew everyone's schedule, waiting by the gate at specific times. He would also be so kind as to walk my brother to the commute stop every morning. After nine years, he disappeared and died of an unknown disease. He left home while he was sick; he did not want us to see him that way. I cried for years and the kids and I still get emotional whenever we remember him. Polo turned out to be one of a kind.

But let me go back to our topic. What was our strategy? A positive reward system. No more and no less. With no dog training background at all, we simply rewarded Polo with a piece of biscuit whenever he followed our request to sit down, shake hands, or lie down. Eventually, he did the tricks without expecting any reward but because he wanted to please us. We established such a strong emotional foundation with him that he did other things apart from what was taught him, such as accompanying me during my morning jogs or trips to the bakery. He even knew whenever I was feeling down; he would just stay within the premises to keep me company even though he was not allowed inside our home.

So before I end up emotional about Polo, what is the relevance of this story? Rapport, emotional foundation, and a positive reward system.

Although this illustration was simple, it has a profound implication to all of us who are molding our children into the best persons they can become.

Here's the relevance:
First and foremost, we specifically identified desirable and undesirable behavior. Shaking of hands, sitting down, pooping outside the house, and staying put. Apart from these, no other behavior was desirable. And as we went along, Polo learned which behavior was desirable or not.

Second, we set up a payoff. In Polo's case, we started with a piece of biscuit and progressed to a tap on the head or a rub on his back. Then, no payoff was given to undesirable behavior.

Third, as mentioned above, we did not start with huge payoffs; neither did we have the same payoff all the time, instead, it came in small steps and quantities until the desired behavior was achieved.

The essence of the positive reward system is that there is always a payoff for desirable behavior. Remember: When a reward or payoff follows an action, that action is likely to be repeated.

Going back to what I mentioned earlier, that most parents use the positive reward system as a form of discipline: Most of them use its exact opposite. They unknowingly reward their children for undesirable behavior, therefore, teaching them undesirable behavior.

THE POSITIVE REWARD SYSTEM

When children behave in a certain way that is acceptable to their parents, such as playing cooperatively with playmates or not whining, parents usually have the tendency to ignore this behavior. It is not at all rewarded. Not a hug or a word of appreciation. Some parents take this desirable behavior for granted. Although it may vary from one child to another, ignoring good behavior results in teaching their children to stop behaving in desirable ways.

But notice what happens when a child acts up. He hits his playmates, throws his food on the floor, steals from his mother, becomes defiant, and does not obey rules. What consequences would result to this? Your guess is as good as mine. For behaving well, he is ignored. But as soon as he acts up otherwise, he immediately gets attention. He is scolded, lectured, spanked, and in ways, given immediate negative attention.

Dr. Fitzhugh Dodson, from whom this book is adapted, has a theory on this: the Law of the Soggy Potato Chip. He says a child prefers a fresh potato chip to a soggy one. But if his choice is between a soggy potato chip or no potato chip at all, he will settle for the soggy one. In the same way, a child prefers a parent's negative attention over no attention at all. For a child, even negative attention is better than being ignored.

Parents may intend negative attention to be a punishment. Strangely enough, studies have shown that it acts as a reward for the child. It is still attention. This is particularly true for children who are hyperactive.

With a positive reward system, we need to be specifically clear with our feelings and actions. By feelings, we refer to internal states of emotion such as love, excitement, anger, fear, frustration, disappointment, or regret. Your child's feelings are his or her private world. There is nothing we can do to change or influence it simply because our children have feelings of their own and their emotions come to their minds instinctively. We can do things we believe will make them happy, but their reaction toward what we do will be entirely up to them.

Many years ago when my son was very young, he would burst into anger when he got into a fight with his other siblings. I gave him space and respected his decision to run up to his room and scream all he wanted (it would, of course, be a different story if he did that while I was talking to him). After respecting his emotions for five to ten minutes, I knocked on his door and helped him process his emotions: what made him angry, was it worth it, questions that would allow him to be more logical about his actions. It is important that we teach our children to understand why they feel the way they do. Afterward, we help them process and assess their behavior without disrespecting their right to feel however they want to feel. Guidance is the key word. We may not have total control over their feelings, but we can teach them how to deal with their emotions.

Next, it is important that we deal only with behaviors that are observable. If you can't see or count the action, it is not subject to parental influence and control. **We need to be**

THE POSITIVE REWARD SYSTEM

specific as to which action or behavior we want to modify or address. If we plainly say, in the case of other children, they don't want to take responsibility, I say for what? When dealing with child behavior, or even adult behavior, **we need to be specific** what THAT behavior is. No vague, motherhood statements. Once we have identified this behavior, then there is something we can work on.

What we must remember about the positive reward system is that a child does not need to show you his good behavior all the time. Say, for example, a child need not keep his closet neat all the time. You can still strengthen this action with positive payoff. Bear mind that, after all, children will be children.

Remember: Positive payoff comes in two forms, the *love payoff* and the *thing payoff*. When we say love payoff, this refers to kisses, praise, hugs, or other forms of physical and verbal affection. Thing payoff obviously refers to tangible items that the child can appreciate. It could be a simple drive-thru at McDonald's for a hot fudge sundae cone, their favorite candy, allowing them to sleep late, to watch their favorite TV show, to bigger things like a new mobile phone or a shopping spree. *<u>This of course would require parents' ability to discern the extent of the reward, keeping in mind their ability to provide such rewards, which should then be commensurate to what the desirable behavior is</u>*. In short, your reward needs to be reasonable. It needs to be commensurate to what you are rewarding. You can't simply reward your child with the newest version of the iPhone just because he or she cleaned their room. Besides, they're supposed to do this anyway.

You also don't need to reward your child every single time. Simply tell them that "special treats are for special times." It is important not to give your child a special treat whenever they ask for it. If you do, you will soon find that you are teaching your child to beg, demand, or be materialistic. Again, parents should be the one in control regarding special treatment. Not the child.

When we reward our children for acceptable behavior, it encourages them to do these things, but the positive effect is on us as well. We unconsciously cultivate the habit of looking for actions we can reward, and not always being on the lookout like a jail guard for mistakes that they've made. Praising our children for good behavior trains us to concentrate more on positive things. That in itself gives us peace in our own disposition.

Before we move on to the next chapter, I would like to clarify a misconception that other parents might have. The positive reward system is not a method to teach our children bribery. A bribe is money or a gift that is given to another person in order for them to do something illegal or immoral. The activities that we are talking about here are not illegal or immoral but a system or method we can use to reinforce a child's good behavior.

Parents who have a well-functioning reward system don't need the other strategies as much. Why? Because there are fewer undesirable behaviors to cope with.

5
THE CONTRACT

In the business world, we are all familiar with contracts. When we buy cars, items for our home, even in retail shops, their official receipts act as a contract that you have agreed to purchase based on the merchant's terms and conditions. It could be a simple no return, no exchange policy or an agreement that you may return the merchandise within a specified period of time.

Therefore, in contracts, there are least two parties. Party A, who promises to do something while Party B promises to do something in return.

As a discipline method at home, contracting is based on the same concept. The contract is between parents and child (or children). The child promises to do (or not to do) a particular thing, and the parent promises to do (or not to do) something in return. To put it another way, if the child changes his behavior in a certain way, the parent will, in turn, change his behavior in a certain way too.

This method of discipline is actually an offshoot of the positive reward system, which works almost unilaterally. It is the parent who decides which behavior can be rewarded and guides their children toward the direction with payoffs. No negotiation is involved. But in contracting, negotiation is an essential element.

Allow me to discuss the process involved in contracting and why it is beneficial for both parent and child (and in any relationship, for that matter).

1. Contracts are mutual agreements resulting from a negotiation process. Both parties have a say on a particular agreement for a situation. It is not just a one-way street.
2. This negotiation results in a commitment on both sides.
3. A commitment binds the two parties. Although, in most cases, the contracts are verbal, there are several reasons why contracts are written down. An agreement in written form prevents misunderstandings and arguments later on. There is a copy for each person, and everybody can see what it does and does not say. For children between the ages of six and twelve, it is psychologically more impressive and ef-

fective to have the contract written down. The more professional and wordy it is to a child of this age, the more it helps them to fulfil their end of the contract.
4. Contracts should be concrete and specific. Actions specified in the contract should be observable and countable. Avoid unclear provisions such as: "Paulina promises to be good." This provision cannot be counted nor can it be specifically observed.
5. The contract should have a positive nature. Rather than contracting so that a child will not do something, create the contract so that the child *will* do something—a desirable behavior. It's like having your own House Rules.

    It is unfortunate that many of us parents state objectives and set ground rules in a negative way. I, for instance, used to tell my youngest daughter, Stephanie: "If you don't finish the food on your plate, you will not have dessert!" I learned, though, that we should present situations to our children in a positive way to encourage them to follow the desirable behavior. Instead, I should have said, "Stephanie, if you finish the food on your plate, you can have dessert right away." I tried it, and it worked! Fast-forward fifteen years, and she is now the successful owner of a cupcake delivery business.
6. The contract must be fair. Both parents and children should end up feeling they made a good deal. If either of the two parties feels that they would be doing too much for what they would be getting,

the contract will somehow end up being sabotaged. Sometimes it is the parent who feels like she is being cheated, and unconsciously ends up making arrangements to take it out on the child.

Generally, it should be up to the parent—as the older and wiser one—to gauge the fairness of the contract. Parents have the ability to look into the future better than the child. The parent should be able to discern how much contribution a child could put into the contract or an agreement for that matter. If a child shows even a hint that they are not agreeable or happy with the contract, it would be advisable to further query their position, whether they find the deal fair enough, or should you make modifications for the child to feel that it's fair.

7. The contract should be designed to be successful. Meaning, parents should be realistic in not expecting a mature or perfect performance from the child in the beginning. We are, after all, dealing with a child. A child's performance will improve once he receives his payoffs and feels more and more positive about the contract. If parents are too optimistic in their expectations, a child is doomed to fail. And if either parent or child does not fulfil their end of the bargain, for whatever reason, then something must have gone wrong physically during the negotiation process.

8. Negotiating skills are not something either parents or children are born with. Even top-notch sales-

men become good at their craft due to the number of years of experience and study. Both parents and child have to learn to negotiate. Since parents have the power, they have to learn to give up some of this power and develop the art of compromise. Since the child has the lesser idea of negotiation and compromise, they will quickly learn this through example from their parents.

When working out a contract, it is important to choose a good time to negotiate. Never try to do it in the heat of the battle or conflict. Contracts should be made rationally and not emotionally (that is precisely the reason why lawyers exist!). However, in our household, the first step in making a contract is for each person to state the problem without "putting down" another party. If we state, for example, "Our problem is that Jett is acting like an obnoxious brat to his little sister," this is certainly a putdown. Instead, we could put it this way: "The problem that we want to work on is that we want Jett to be more tolerant and patient with his little sister, especially whenever she asks for help." There is an objective and it is not at all a putdown. We then work on a compromise which may be the solution: "It would help Jett to be patient if you, Stephanie, would not speak too loudly in his ear and half an inch from his face whenever you ask for assistance."

Apart from teaching our children good behavior from contracting, we are also providing them the necessary training in the art of negotiation and compromise. This will be of immense help to them later on in the adult world. Once your children become accustomed to contracting, you may eventually find them taking the initiative in suggesting contracts to you for things that they really want.

With younger children (five years and below), the contract should not extend longer than the day you work it out. With children six to twelve, it can extend as long as a week or longer depending on the child. For teenagers, the length of the contract can follow the breaks in the school year, several weeks or even months. When the behavior with which you are concerned is under control, you would then no longer need a formal contract. You can then gradually fade out payoffs in the positive reward system.

> The most important trip you may take in life is meeting people halfway.
>
> Henry Boye

6

TIME-OUT, REVERSE TIME-OUT, AND PHYSICAL RESTRAINT

It is suggested that punishment should be eliminated as a way of dealing with the undesirable behavior of a child.

We can do this by first eliminating the payoffs for undesirable behavior. This method may be used for behavior that does not harm the child or others, does not destroy, or simply does not get on your nerves.

When we say we should eliminate payoffs for undesirable behavior, this is because for every undesirable behavior, our child is somewhere, somehow, getting some payoff. It is our job to find and eliminate this payoff. The ability to discern is essential.

Let me give you an example. Every time we ate dinner, my daughter had a habit of sitting far from the table. Not only was it improper to sit that way; it was also causing the food to spill on her clothes and all over the place. This bothered me so much that every time we ate dinner, I had to constantly tell her to sit properly, like a lady would, considering that she was the eldest and was almost a teenager.

Then a psychiatrist friend of mine suggested that I eliminate the payoff. I realized then that the payoff was the constant attention—no matter how annoying this could be for her too (remember the law of the soggy potato chip?).

So the next time we had dinner, she sat the same way, but I tried hard not to utter a word. I was clasping both my hands under the table to get a grip on myself and control my irritation while I was bleeding internally. The whole time, she kept glancing at me as if waiting for me to say something about how she was seated. Before the end of our meal, she called my attention to tell me that she was seated differently from her other siblings. I just smiled and said:

TIME-OUT, REVERSE TIME-OUT, AND PHYSICAL RESTRAINT

"I know." "Aren't you going to say something?" she asked. "No," I replied.

This behavior went on for several more evenings, with me keeping silent. On the tenth night, I was amazed that she sat for dinner just like her other siblings did. So there you go, one undesirable behavior curtailed.

Another classic example was when my son was only four years old. There was a time when he would come home with new four-letter words that really freaked me out. Each time he came home, he would try out these words to me and seem to be amused with my usual reaction, which was to get up from my seat and start giving him a run-through of why he shouldn't say that word.

Remembering to eliminate the payoffs, I realized, *I am the adult and I should be the one in control of the situation. Not the one freaking out.* So the next time my son came to me to try out those words again. I stayed as calm as I could and told him, "That's a bad word, sweetheart. Please don't say it again." Eventually, his trying-out habit faded away.

I must emphasize, though, that children (and adults, for that matter) cannot change their behavior overnight. Which is why we have to keep in mind that it takes a lot of patience and dedication to mold our children into the better persons we want them to be.

Removing payoffs works for all types of undesirable behavior, except for actions that fall into these three categories I mentioned earlier:

1. Actions that may hurt or endanger the child or someone else (obviously, it is not wise to ignore this behavior if a child, for example, is about to hit another child)
2. Actions that will destroy property (throwing unpaid-for items at the grocery, writing on the wall, spitting at people)
3. Actions that are not dangerous but for some reason get on your nerves or seriously distract you (for example, you're driving and your child keeps singing "Twinkle, Twinkle, Little Star," even after an hour or so—I'm sure any parent would feel exasperated)

What alternative do we have in the above categories? A time-out, which by far is the most effective and widely used discipline tool in North America and Europe. However, since most parents confuse time-out with sending children to their rooms, here are some guidelines as to how a time-out is really supposed to work:

1. Keep in mind that the time-out technique is not really a punishment. Say, for example, your child is about to hit another child. You say, "Honey, I cannot let you hit your playmate. I think you need a time-out. For your time-out, you should go to your room and stay there for five minutes. I will let you know when the five minutes are up." (If your child does not have his own room or you are not in your home, you may send him to a place where he can be alone yet remain safe and secure.)

One of the advantages of the time-out is that you

TIME-OUT, REVERSE TIME-OUT, AND PHYSICAL RESTRAINT

have geographically disrupted the undesirable behavior. He cannot hit other children if he is physically taken away from the situation. This means that each time your child presents undesirable behavior, you can geographically disrupt it by means of a time-out.

2. Since time-out is not a punishment, it does not violate the law of the soggy potato chip. The time-out is simply a bland, boring five minutes in which nothing exactly happens.

Remember: The time-out should be administered in a cool, calm, collected, and prompt manner. That means you do not tell a child to stop doing something twelve times and then give the time-out. No one remains cool, calm, and collected that way. Once the five minutes or time you've allotted for the time-out are over, do not announce that the child can leave their room already. Instead, simply announce that the five-minute time-out is over.

3. Time-out is valuable because it is a versatile discipline technique. It can be used with two or more children, putting each of them in separate rooms or in similar locations. This is particularly helpful for bickering or fighting between siblings.

    With the time-out, parents can prevent what I call a "courtroom drama" where I have to play judge and prosecutor and determine who started what. I simply express to the children that they need a time-out and I'll announce when the five minutes are up. I impress upon them that I don't need to figure out who started it.

A friend of mine asked me why I need not find out who started it. My philosophy in this is that later on, as they become adults and they are faced with real-life issues, there will be more circumstances wherein who initiated what first will be of lesser importance than how they deal with the situation. It teaches them that fighting or bickering is not the answer.

4. Others perceive the time-out technique as a tool more beneficial for the parents. Some parents feel more comfortable and self-confident in dealing with their children's misbehavior this way. This discipline method may be used for children at about age three to twelve.

Note: There are some parents who encounter a special difficulty when their younger children refuse to take the time-out. (This poses a larger problem when the parents have not established their authority at home. We will discuss this later on in another chapter). If a child defies a parent's request to go to their room, the parent should escort the child physically to the room, even if the child is kicking or screaming, get the child inside, and close the door (make sure that the room is safe). The parent should stand outside the door, in silence, holding the knob firmly to keep the door closed for the required five minutes. Depending on how stubborn the child is, it may take several days or weeks for the child to realize that there is no sense in fighting the time-out. For once a time-out has been called, the child is going to the

TIME-OUT, REVERSE TIME-OUT, AND PHYSICAL RESTRAINT

room and will stay there for five minutes.

Although time-out is recommended for children three years or older, it is not suitable for very young children (eighteen months to two years) and is particularly ill-suited for children whose language development is very limited. That is why this next discipline technique is for parents or caretakers of very young children. It is called the reverse time-out. In this case, instead of isolating the child as in the time-out, it is the parent who is isolated.

This is how it works. Once you feel that you've had it for the moment—cries, entreaties, throwing of toys, or whatever kind of tantrum—instead of sending a child to their room for a time-out, put yourself in a room where the child cannot get to you. Take a book, retreat to the bathroom, and lock the door. Once you are in your chosen room, do not respond to the child in any way (of course you have to make sure that the child is in a safe environment).

Be especially careful not to give in even if the child has been banging the door for twenty minutes or so. Remember Charlotte in the movie *Sex in the City,* when she lost it after being overwhelmed with a crying baby and a four-year-old stamping her vintage skirt with red icing? She went inside the pantry. Her daughter was banging on the door and all she said was: "Sweetie, give Mommy a few minute please..." And there, she cried her heart out while speaking on the phone with her best friend. Once she composed herself, she went right back out.

If you give in to your child during these moments where you need space, you are giving her a very powerful payoff to keep banging the door until you open up the next time you decide you need a time-out.

You have to wait for the child to give up, until the atmosphere is calm and peaceful outside. This is the behavior you want to promote. This is the only time you give a payoff by opening the door, when the child is already calm (and perhaps tired). But if you come out and the child starts acting up again, go back to your room or the bathroom until the child learns to control their behavior. (Note: Not applicable for children with special needs.)

DO NOT USE THE REVERSE TIME-OUT AS A THREAT. If you have the need for a reverse time-out, simply do it. But don't hold it over a child's head as a means to threaten them and make them feel that they will be left alone. Because reality is, you are only in the next room.

Studies have shown that these techniques have proven to decrease the rate of parents hitting their children and afterward feeling sorry they did it.

Another method of dealing with undesirable behavior is through physical restraint of the child. No, we will not tie up our children or put cuffs on them just so they won't hit us or the other kids. This mainly pertains to emergency situations where the time-out technique is not fast enough. Say, for example, your child is about to poke a playmate in the eye with a sharp stick. You run over and grab the stick out

TIME-OUT, REVERSE TIME-OUT, AND PHYSICAL RESTRAINT

of the child's hand. Hold the child's arm firmly with both your hands and say to him loudly: "Sticks are for playing in the sand or digging dirt; they are not for stabbing or hitting people."

Another common example is when a child throws a tantrum and their temper seems impossible to control through a time-out. Approach your child and sweep him up into your arms and immobilize him until his temper subsides (make sure he is not squeezed too tight; just encase him in your arms). As you do this, tell your child: "You're so angry I have to hold you tight until you feel better. You might end up hurting yourself or other people."

What this technique is trying to tell us is that we need to use our common sense. We need to use a technique that embodies swift emergency actions rather than one that is leisurely.

7

ENVIRONMENTAL CONTROL

Many parents miss out on the fact that controlling a child's environment is one of the essential factors to effectively discipline a child, thereby creating fewer problems for themselves. This is why preschoolers seldom show negative behavior on a well-designed playground. They are happy and pleasant because the environment is adapted to their age level.

This is also why some of the biggest interior design concepts are called no-no designs. Some newly married couples who design their homes do not consider the necessity of changing the environment when a child becomes a part of their

ENVIRONMENTAL CONTROL

new life together.

This principle is very simple. You must control your child's environment so that there is little they can do in the way of undesirable behavior. If his environment is filled with things that would tempt him (say, for example, your most expensive set of shiny crystal on the coffee table), trouble will follow.

The moral of environmental control is this: When confronted with misbehavior, ask yourself this question: Is there anything I can change in my child's environment that will eliminate the problem? If there is, change it. Simply put, environmental control is preventive discipline. I need to emphasize though that environmental control does not only refer to structure. It also refers to people you choose to surround your children with. No well-meaning parent would consciously want their child to be surrounded by cursing, alcoholic, or drug-taking individuals. Some parents even move to a different location to ensure that they raise their children in a conducive neighborhood.

Next is the principle of natural consequences, wherein a parent allows unpleasant but natural consequences to happen when a child does not act in a desirable manner.

A good example would be this: A parent once approached me because she was greatly disturbed by the behavior of her son during mealtime. The child would constantly play with his glass to the point that both parents would jump off their seats, as they feared that the water might spill on the child.

CHILDREN DON'T COME WITH A MANUAL

This became so embarrassing that the child would do it with visitors around.

I suggested that the next time the child does this, they only tell him once that if he does not stop playing with his glass, the water will spill on him.

The next time the child played with his glass of water, the parents reminded the child of the possible consequence of his action only once. And as the natural law of consequence had it, the water did spill on the child, resulting in a soaked cold shirt. The parents just looked at him as the child sat in a bit of a shock. The parents then asked the child to go to his room and change his clothes. After a couple more incidents like this, the child learned that it is more advisable to behave and not play with his glass than to have to leave the table, dry himself, and change the clothes.

The basic principle of natural consequences is to let your child learn from experiences, wherever possible, where it cannot result in serious injury. If the natural consequences are pleasant, the child will continue to act that way. If the natural consequences are unpleasant, the child will be motivated to change his actions.

We have to teach our children the concept that we will not always be around to protect them. Once they are on their own in the real world, they have to make choices and be able to <u>discern</u> which consequences would be appropriate. They learn to take care of themselves by learning the natural consequences of their actions. This greatly helps in the development of their self-confidence and self-esteem.

8
TO SPANK OR NOT TO SPANK, THAT IS THE QUESTION

If asked what chapter in this book I had difficulty writing, I would have to say this one.

In my son's earlier years, he had a bout with anger management. He would easily be angered and the intensity of his resentment would not be commensurate to the situation at hand. More often than not, he would be screaming and kicking. He would growl and grunt like a warrior about to be put in the ring, ready for a match.

Seeing your son at five having that much anger is very disconcerting. Although the strangest thing was that he never,

ever vented on me (usually his little sister was the clueless casualty—she was three at that time). I attribute this now to rapport. Yet still, this behavior was unacceptable and undesirable.

My usual approach when he was in this mode was to simply speak to him. Just like any negotiator, I told him that I understood his frustration. I made it a point that he did not to go to bed without taking responsibility for his actions. I asked him to write five things that he thought he did wrong that particular moment.

He wrote about his "unbecoming behavior" and how sorry he was. I was happy with that since my son had this mindset of carrying up to the following day any disappointment or frustration he had the day before.

His father chanced upon him the following morning picking on his younger sister, again. His father was always patient but perhaps realized that the behavior his son showed his little sister had reached its limit and was no longer acceptable. In short, he gave him a big whack on the butt. One of the very few times he ever did.

Spanking is such a widely used form of punishment (read: not discipline but punishment). A lot of books have been written about the pros and cons of spanking. Most psychiatrists and psychologists explicitly state that no parent should ever spank a child. I believe it's unrealistic to think this way.

Say, for example, you are a well-meaning parent who was advised that a no-spanking policy should exist in your home.

TO SPANK OR NOT TO SPANK, THAT IS THE QUESTION

You have a child who has been misbehaving badly and you have been longing to give him a spank. But then, you believe in the book, that you will become a terrible parent if you are one of the parents who spanks their children. So you muster enough self-control and don't spank your child. The result? The tension between you and your child becomes stronger as the number of times you dread to give your child a spanking but stop yourself from doing so. That's why this approach is unrealistic. It would be better that you give your child a few swats to clear the air. Afterward, the two of you can start over again. I perceive this as the same concept in adults wherein you try to bring a hysterical person back to reality by giving them one big slap. Afterward, one feels sorry but is able to release tension, and the other becomes more in touch with the world and realizes that they can't always have it their way.

Again, I will emphasize that spanking is a poor and less effective method of teaching. If parents were perfect, then there would be no need for spanking at all. But we are not. We are human beings whose patience has limits, we have tempers. Oftentimes, we show our humanity by being the vulnerable and affected people that we are. Which is why I make room for the occasional spanking, not because it is a good form of discipline strategy, but because it is an integral part of human nature and for my children to realize that I have limits too.

I'll try to recall the number of times I have given my children a spanking throughout my life: My eldest, about seven times. My son, cannot remember. My youngest, only once as well. But she remembers it vividly, that it did not even really hurt; she was just surprised that I attempted to spank her. And if I recall it accurately, I have not spanked any of them since they were four or five years old. When I did so, I was a young mother in my twenties. I did not have the tolerance nor patience that I do now.

Children have their own characteristics and personalities. I figure now that perhaps the reason I spanked my youngest less than the other two children was because she was an easier child to deal with. And by my third child, I knew better how to handle my children. Obviously, spanking is not a widely used form of discipline for me. And when I say spanking, I mean, a few swats with a slipper on your child's bottom. To spank or hit them in another part of their body is unreasonable. I don't use my hands either. Children should not learn to identify your hands as a tool that will inflict pain on them. This is why I use a slipper since it is a detached object that can be discarded later on. Above all, we teach children to love, and one of our greatest tools to show love is our hands. Hands are for showing love, not pain.

If the other strategies in this book are used properly, you will find that there are fewer times of frustration that will give you the emotional need to spank. And I am sure you would like to spank as seldom as possible. Since spanking is a punishment and not a form of discipline, it suffers from many psychological drawbacks that go with any form of punishment.

TO SPANK OR NOT TO SPANK, THAT IS THE QUESTION

I reiterate, whenever we spank a child, it teaches them to hate, fear, and avoid us. The number of times we spank them is the equivalent amount of hate, fear, and wanting to avoid us they will feel. How can we become good and effective examples and teachers to our children if they fear and avoid us or, more so, if they hate us? It has also been proven by many studies that spanking arouses a deep desire in children to retaliate and seek revenge as they get older.

Spanking, like other forms of punishment, is useless as the child gets older, say eleven or twelve (in girls, when they start having their monthly period). Come to think of it, how could one possibly spank a teenager unless they're a father who is as huge as Arnold Schwarzenegger, or a mother as strong and powerful as Xena, the warrior princess? (I assure you, even Arnie and Xena cannot prevent their children from running away after being spanked!)

> **My parents spanked me as a child**
>
> **As a result I now suffer from a psychological condition known as "Respect for Others"**

9
THE FEEDBACK TECHNIQUE

In the earlier chapters, we discussed techniques to handle our children's actions. Now, let us discuss how to handle our children's feelings. To define, feelings are internal states within our child's mind such as fear, joy, love, excitement, sadness, and anger. We cannot control feelings. They come into our minds voluntarily. We cannot will them. But actions are different. A child can control his actions (unless he is younger, say, a year old, he can be in the process of learning to control his actions). For example, your child cannot help feeling angry after his younger brother tore apart his precious mechanical toy, but he can keep himself from hitting or punching him. Because of the huge disparity between feelings and actions, we as parents need to handle these two differently.

THE FEEDBACK TECHNIQUE

Parents should encourage their children to express their feelings. To rephrase, parents should <u>allow</u> and encourage their children to express their feelings. Be it positive or negative, they should be taught to express their feelings in words or in other productive forms. I, for instance, have taught my son, who easily gets wound up and irritable, a couple of words to express his feelings: *I am disappointed. I feel unhappy. I don't feel comfortable.* It is best that we teach them how to express negative emotions in these acceptable words rather than cursing. Positive feelings are much easier to find words for than negative feelings, so children must be taught to express negative feelings in this manner. Just the same way we teach them to express all their feelings in words.

My children see that another outlet for me to express a negative feeling is through my crafts, art works, baking, and writing. Although, we need to explain that it does not necessarily follow that when I do these things, I am feeling bad. We should show them that feelings, good or bad, are energies that need to be manifested in a positive way.

I am a strong advocate for encouraging children to express their feelings, negative and positive alike. Let me tell you why.

1. When children are allowed to express their feelings, particularly their negative feelings, it's like a safety valve on a boiler which prevents it from exploding. Allowing a child to express their feelings prevents them from exploding also.
2. If a child regularly bottles up their feelings, it is dif-

ficult to get this out of their system as they grow up. Eventually, it will be difficult for them to take in positive feelings. Perhaps this is another reason why some people are negativistic.

During my younger years, our father taught us that children should be seen and not heard. Imagine, with my innate loquacious personality, I was not allowed to say what was on my mind most of the time! Fortunately, my life experiences and education have allowed me to relearn these things.

3. A young child, in particular, like some adults, does not have the ability to compartmentalize their feelings. They are unable to hold back only the negative feelings without pushing down positive feelings as well.

   I remember an experience with an eight-year-old child who once attended a baking class I conducted with my then eight-year-old daughter. As part of my teaching style, I allow the children to handle the baking tools and take turns mixing the batter. In this process, the children end up making a mess on the floor and their aprons. The child whispered to me, asking why I was allowing the other students to make a mess in the kitchen. She said, "This is precisely the reason why most children are irresponsible."

   It was sad to hear a child speak and think that way. Although she spoke in the voice of a child, her choice of words and the essence of what she was

THE FEEDBACK TECHNIQUE

saying were definitely not for her age. What she said concerned me because she spoke of the other children as if she herself was not a child. I said to myself, *This child thinks she is a miniaturized adult.*

4. If a child, or even an adult for that matter, evokes antisocial forms of behavior, it will be difficult for them to express their negative feelings in words. This makes me remember an incident when I was about seven and my younger brother was only four. Since I was much bigger than he was at that time, I would always take things from him casually, be it a piece of bread or toy. He seldom uttered a word whenever I did this, which is why I thought it was no big deal. One day, I saw my precious Barbie doll drowning in the toilet bowl.

Furious as I was, I thought hard as to who could have done this horrible deed to my "best friend." After a long thought, I eliminated from my list of "suspects" my parents (they were at work), my nanny (she knew how important Barbie was to me and would even dress her up while I was away on trips), my older sister (she valued our toys too much; her own toys were still in plastic wrapping). Not the driver, not the gardener, neither could it be the neighbor's kids (not that they could go in the house without an invitation). It couldn't have been anyone else but my four-year-old brother! Raging mad, I went up to his room holding my precious doll, whose hair was soaked in toilet bowl water. I said: "Why on earth did you try to hurt my dolly? Are you mad at me?" He then said: "Well, you always get my bread…" I had no idea he felt that way about me. But before hell could break loose, my mama came into the picture and explained to my brother: "If you're feeling bad about something, you have to let us know." It was a simple rule my mom made among us siblings, but its long-term effects were significant.

5. Children who are not taught or allowed to express their negative feelings end up as adults who also cannot express negative feelings. A psychiatrist friend of mine, Dr. Rommel Papa of the National Bureau of Investigation, told me that in his many years of practice, a huge percentage of his patients suffering from anxiety attacks and depression have been known to have repressed anger or sexual feelings. But once they are able to exorcise these repressed, angry feelings, they eventually overcome their anxiety and depression.

These days, modern parenting style encourages us to give our children the freedom to express their feelings in words. This is considered one of the greatest gifts we can give to our children. However, it also has its drawbacks:

> One, we are worried that in as much as expressing their feelings in words is acceptable at home, people outside your home might find it offensive or disrespectful. My answer to that is: in the process of teaching our children to express their feel-

THE FEEDBACK TECHNIQUE

ings, we should also teach them to distinguish when and where it is safe to do so. Remember our chapter "The Parent As the Parent"?

Two, we know for a fact that allowing our children to speak freely about their thoughts and feelings is both mentally and emotionally healthy, but sometimes a deep voice inside of me still says: "Don't you dare talk to me that way. I'm still your mother!" most especially if the manner in which they respond is not acceptable. This of course is not the voice inside of me that is a psychologist. This is the voice of my father from the past, reminding me that children should be seen and not heard. I have to admit that there is no ready solution to this but to keep on working to overcome our own childhood hang-ups.

Whenever I give talks on child behavior and discipline, it is almost always certain that I will be asked: "What about respect for parents?" My answer: Most people misconstrue respect as keeping your disgust or anger with others to yourself. Well, if that is respect, I don't see what good it does to anybody. Respect, according to Mr. Webster, is to have regard for, to treat with propriety or with consideration. Taking this definition and applying it to parenting, a child respects a parent when the child is aware that the parent knows more about life than she does and that the parent is a person of integrity to whom she can look for guidance. In the military and police academy, we call this moral ascendancy. I believe that allowing a child to express their feelings only affects their respectfulness depending on the manner in which they choose to express it.

Children need to be understood. Not that parents are cruel or unfeeling, but most of the time, they are unable to let their children know that they understand how they feel because no one has taught them how to convey this kind of understanding. Also, many parents have not learned the importance of listening to their children and empathizing with them.

The feedback technique allows the child to know that the parent is exerting an effort to understand them because the child will hear her own feelings being expressed by her parent. Bear in mind that, when using this technique, you do not sound like an echo. You need to rephrase your child's feelings in your own words. Again, bear in mind that he will not always make an outward response. But every time you feed back his feelings, he will know that Mommy or Daddy understands him. That it is a good thing to express what you feel and think at the right moment. Do not expect a dramatic change to take place in the child as a result of this technique. Remember: the outcome of the techniques discussed in this book varies from child to child.

10
THE MUTUAL PROBLEM-SOLVING TECHNIQUE

Every family has conflicts between what a child wants, what the parent wants, and what the parent allows their children to do.

Most of these conflicts may be resolved by the discipline techniques we have discussed earlier. However, bear in mind that as the child grows older, some of the techniques are no longer as effective compared to when they were younger—most especially when they have reached adolescence. They lose their instinctive fear of punishment. Instead, most of them think: "I'll be punished again for my unacceptable behavior; let's see if I care!"

Again, let me emphasize that this is not the stage where our children transform into little monsters whose objectives are to make us feel eternally bad. Fact is, our children are in the stage (between the ages of twelve to thirteen) of development where their developmental task is to form an ego identity that is different from one's parent. That is why parents who have children in their early adolescence are often heard saying: "Your dad and I never taught you that" or "I wonder where you got that attitude?"

We shall discuss more about this in the latter part of the book. This will enable us to understand the different developmental stages that our children go through.

When parent power consistently loses and the child power consistently wins (say, for instance, most of us would give in to what a child wants just to avoid any confrontation, or in some cases, the parents are firm in their ground rules but the child disregards them anyway), the parents become furious at the child and hate themselves for not being able to stand up to their child and their demands. They feel ashamed for not being able to assert themselves.

There is, however, an effective alternative to avoid the power struggles between the parent and the child: the mutual problem-solving technique. In this technique, both sides win and nobody loses.

1. The parent and child conflict must be clearly identified. The child wants one thing and the parent wants something else. That is the issue that needs to be resolved.
2. Whoever is involved in the issue must agree to find a solution. It could be a parent and a child; two parents and a child; two children and the parents;

THE MUTUAL PROBLEM-SOLVING TECHNIQUE

      two children and a parent, or whatever the structure may be.
3. Those who are involved in the conflict or issue must appoint a note taker. That person's job is to simply jot down whatever ideas come forth as a solution to the problem.
4. Those involved should engage in brainstorming. This term and technique was discovered by Dr. Alex Osborn. He first applied this strategy to generate ideas in solving business problems. He pointed out that where three or four people sit down to solve a problem, it is likely that someone will say that the idea will not work because…and the net effect is to inhibit people from coming up with new ideas.

The first rule of brainstorming is that no one is allowed to criticize anybody else's idea. Everyone should be encouraged to come up with an idea—no matter how silly or far out it may sound.

Explain to your family how brainstorming works. After assigning a note taker, make sure that you do not brainstorm over twenty minutes or under five minutes.

Once all the ideas have been written down, go over them one by one and try to find the best solution to the problem. The solution should be one that everybody agrees on. If even one person disagrees with the idea, it should be discarded. There should also be no voting, because in voting, someone wins and someone loses. That is not our objective.

Mutual problem solving should have a unanimous

agreement; thereby, everybody wins and nobody loses. Everybody will be much more highly motivated to see the decision carried out if they are part of the decision-making process.

This method of settling disputes is not new. As a matter of fact, many companies use this strategy in labor and management conflicts. Many companies who do not resolve issues in this manner are those with the most labor and management problems. Even marriages—do you think any spouse would consider himself or herself happily married if their marriages operated on their spouse's imposing power?

This technique may be used with children after the age of five. During ages five to ten, it is recommended that it be reserved for more complex problems, although from eleven onward, this technique becomes very helpful, particularly during the teenage years.

In mutual problem solving, the advantage is both for the parents and the children:

One, it promotes a deeper relationship between parent and child since everybody wins and nobody loses.

Two, children are taught and motivated to carry out solutions to certain issues and problems by participating in the problem solving process. The solutions to the problems were not forced upon them.

Three, the use of this problem – solving technique develops thinking skills in children. Later on in their adult years, they

THE MUTUAL PROBLEM-SOLVING TECHNIQUE

will carry on this attitude on how to deal with the realities of life itself.

Four, the use of this technique reduces hostility on the part of the child, and sometimes, the parent. Since both parties need to agree to a solution, no one is likely to walk away angry as they are conditioned to conform to the processes of solving the problem rather than secretly plotting to sabotage a solution that they were never involved resolving in the first place.

Lastly, since it is a process, the use of this technique often gets below the surface of what the "real" problem really is. As the parent and child discuss the problem from their own perspectives, it becomes clear which areas of concern are really bothering the child.

One final word though. If you have carefully tried this technique as outlined in this chapter, and results only in dismal failure, then something is probably wrong in the way it is executed, or perhaps, even bigger problems are causing the failure of the technique. I would then suggest that a professional be consulted to find out why this technique is not working for you.

Mutual problem-solving is only new when applied to parent-child relationships. This is simply because few parents sit down with their children to solve conflicts in this manner. Some parents who are aware of this method sometimes forget to use this technique, especially when our pride starts to overcome us.

CHILDREN DON'T COME WITH A MANUAL

We have to constantly remind ourselves that children are only transient in our lives and that what they will become in the future is a reflection of our life's work as a parent. More important than any achievement any parent can have and acquire in this lifetime.

THE ONLY THING THAT WILL REDEEM MANKIND IS COOPERATION

BERTRAND RUSSELL

PICTUREQUOTES.com

11
THE FAMILY COUNCIL

The family council is often referred to as the extension of the problem-solving technique. In this case, it involves all the family members, including the youngest children (although they may be excluded if they prove to be disruptive during the problem-solving process).

This technique, however, is not new to most Asian families or families that operate as a clan. The family council requires regular meetings at least once a week. Since most Asian families are accustomed to meet every week either for a Sunday brunch or dinner, this is not a difficult task.

As in every family gathering, missed meetings destroy continuity and the feeling of cohesiveness that is built up over the course of time during council meetings. This is also the time when members of the family are able to update the other members with what has been going on with their lives. It actually becomes a venue to get to know the other members a little better. Do not, however, misconstrue this as a gathering where people gossip or rumor – monger about each other. This is, to begin with, your family.

The first order of the day is to appoint a chairman, who is usually, but not necessarily, the eldest in the family. The position rotates every week.

The principle of freedom, not coercion, is used. No one is forced to attend the meeting of the family council, and any member may leave the meeting at any time.

So, how do you prevent persons from disrupting the family council? In the most unusual way. When someone is annoying and starts to disrupt the meeting, anyone who is reasonably annoyed can leave the meeting. Also, when a member disrupts the meeting, only the chairman can request the person to behave accordingly. If he does not behave, then others in the meeting may decide to leave.

During the meeting, anyone in the council may bring up anything they wish to talk about. Anything. From problems, conflicts, difficulties, grievances, and even plans for an outing.

However, what is brought up must be a matter of common concern for the entire family. It should not be something that is strictly for specific family members.

As with the mutual problem-solving technique, there must be a unanimous agreement on the solution to the problem. Again, there should be no voting, because in voting,

THE FAMILY COUNCIL

someone wins and someone loses. And those who lose will become disgruntled and won't be motivated to carry out the solution to the issue. If a unanimous agreement cannot be derived from the meeting, try again the next meeting.

The family council is a proficient way for children to air resentments and get grievances off their chests before they build into major problems in the future. And whenever there are grievances and resentments, the feedback technique should be used.

As mentioned earlier, the family council is not just a venue to solve problems and air grievances. It should also be a place to make plans for outings, trips, family vacations and activities. You then appreciate that the decisions derived from the family council are acquired in a democratic manner by one or both parents.

Not sure how to begin?

First, the parent should talk about the concept thoroughly. You have to realize that if you decide to adopt such a procedure, a risk is being undertaken. This is the risk of letting democracy into your family structure. Although the parents are, and should still be in authority, children are given the privilege of speaking out their thoughts and ideas. This is a situation where parents sometimes feel that the situation becomes uncontrollable and the line between authority and democracy becomes a gray area.

Once you have decided that you have a good grasp of the family council technique as well as its structure, present the idea to your family. Tell the children that you would have an organized meeting wherein each member of the family would be given the opportunity to speak their thoughts, ideas, and grievances. But emphasize that the decisions, resolutions, or solutions derived from the family council will not be from mom or dad alone but from a unanimous agreement from all the family members.

It is suggested that meetings should be short at first (about fifteen minutes), and then later on, half an hour, forty-five minutes, as the time is needed. But as experts have learned, when you have a family with teenagers, meetings become quite lengthy as they discuss certain issues.

The advantage of having a family council is that it helps give family members a venue to settle grievances and conflicts within the family. However, that is very minor compared to the training that the children will get from the art of human relations. It equips them with the ability to address issues at the proper venue and to the right persons. It also teaches them the value of their family's outputs when they make bigger decisions in the future.

When you start training your child at the age of three regarding the mechanics of the family council, by the time he is eighteen, he already has fifteen solid years of training in learning to adjust, understand, and get along with the other members of the family. This learning experience is then carried on in his adult life when he is faced with human relation experiences as well as decision making. And since the position of the chairman rotates with each family member, he will have plenty of time to learn to reconcile others with opposing points of view as well as enough patience and practice as secretary to properly analyze issues being discussed during the meeting.

12
PARENTAL MUSCLE

Parental muscle is the sheer raw power on the part of the parents.

I do not believe in the use of power itself. It is immoral and bad when used excessively. It must not be misconstrued as privileges, entitlement, and opportunity. As it is clearly underlined in this book, mutual agreement is far more superior to imposing power either by the parent or the child. It is also clear in this book that negotiation and agreement are the more recommendable techniques in solving problems and conflicts than through power.

This chapter is what I would refer to as the last recourse. And because I have learned that families, particularly those with teenagers, have found it necessary to use this technique, I would feel negligent to leave it out.

In extreme cases, when all resources have been tried and have failed, I agree with other experts that we need to fall back on sheer power to bring order out of chaos in the lives of our children and the people who are affected in their lives.

A word of caution though. Parents should first consult a professional before they fall back on parental muscle. A book can only talk about children or families in general, but a professional therapist can deal with your children in a more individualized approach which no other self-help books can.

So before applying any drastic actions mentioned in this chapter, consult a professional.

When drastic measures are undertaken, it almost always involves families with teenagers. It is very rare that young children defy parental authority in outrageous ways.

Let me cite an example for a clearer picture. I had a former colleague who would often come up to me crying about her children's lack of consideration. She's a working mother while her husband is out of the country as an overseas worker.

Since she is left alone to take care of the children and run the household, her children, ages eighteen, sixteen, and fourteen, are expected to help keep house, right? No. The only responsibility they see for themselves is to study. Their rooms are a mess, they don't help fix the table during meals, nor do they help in the kitchen. Whenever their mother tells them to help with the chores, they start frowning and making faces.

Finally, my colleague told me that she'd had it. She couldn't bear all the responsibilities in running the house by herself, and all three children did not even bother to help! So, she stopped buying the groceries. She spent more time at work not only to get more things done but because she needed to show the children that they need to help in the house and that the chores are not for their mother alone. She also stopped cleaning the house since they were also the ones who didn't tidy it up after making a mess whenever they had visitors. And since she purposely went home late, so was their dinner.

At first, the children tried to outsmart her by scrounging food at their grandmother's house until it became too embarrassing to do so every day. Takeout became too expensive to be a way of life as well. They also realized what a mess the house was without Mom cleaning up after them. They had to face the fact that their mother controlled the finances and that they also had to take responsibility in running the house as a family.

I told my colleague not to approach the children but instead to wait for them to come to her. And finally, after two weeks, they came to her and said they wanted to have a discussion. Of course the discussion was heated and heavy, but

PARENTAL MUSCLE

Mother stood her ground. The resolution: They all agreed to write down what chore they could contribute to keep house. Since one was very much into eating, she was assigned to help in the kitchen while their mother cooks; the two other children divided between them the other chores since they usually had visitors for study groups. Finally, the burden wasn't with the mother alone. Keeping the house was a family effort, and it was clear what their responsibilities and participation were.

Let me give you a more extreme example. A co-parent from my daughter's school came to me asking for assistance. She wanted to know how to get her much older son into rehabilitation. In many Asian countries, sons are regarded with high esteem and importance as they carry their father's name.

She had an eighteen-year-old son who had been kicked out from school because he was caught taking and influencing the use of drugs to other students. Since he was no longer in school and his parents found it difficult to look for another school in the middle of the year, he spent most of the time at home, lying around and high on drugs. His parents both worked and would not be able to monitor him twenty-four hours a day.

They had used practically every discipline technique I have known. As a matter of fact, the other four children did well in school and were courteous and respectful. I must say, they were very good people as well, except for this particular son, who had caused them terrible heartache and embarrassment.

Nothing seemed to work. They had even seen a therapist but eventually dropped off after three sessions.

Finally, the boy's father made a decision. "He doesn't want to go to school, and neither does he want to get a job in the meantime. He is stoned most of the time. We need to send him to a rehab." The mother was shocked. This meant not seeing their son for a couple of months, and the thought of him living differently and comfortably from what he was used to just broke her heart.

The father gave his son one more week to get his act together. He spoke to him and told him about the ultimatum. Yet, a week passed and nothing seemed to change.

To cut the long story short, we arranged for an ambulance to pick him up from their home and take him straight into rehab. The parents had signed all the necessary documents and only saw their son after three months. After a year and a half, he finally graduated from a computer programming school and was being eyed by a company to work overseas.

If you would ask me what the turning point was, it was when his parents decided he should be out of the house to seek professional help. Yes, they felt sad that he had to leave, most especially his mother, who was very gentle and loving, but in the long term, it was for his own good.

What am I trying to say in this chapter? Younger children rarely need to be taught in this manner. Even with other teenagers, the feedback technique, mutual problem-solving technique, family council, and other discipline methods mentioned in this book are usually sufficient to handle any behavioral concern. If these methods do not take care of things, then the family should see a professional. But again, you must remember that results do not happen overnight.

Unlike other discipline books, I included this method because most books stress the importance of active listening, where parents ask their children to sit down and talk about issues, but I have yet to see a book that tells you what to do when your child starts screaming at you and says, "Shut up!" and refuses to talk about the problem.

My point is, extreme cases of defiance of parental authority should have an equivalent measure of parental muscle that will be of leverage to the defiant child.

Using parental power is like performing major neurosurgery. It should not be done in haste or taken ill-advisedly or lightly. It is a serious remedial measure that should be done only when necessary and with proper advice.

13
TEACHING OUR CHILDREN ETHICS AND MORALITY

Contrary to common belief, children are not born with a conscience. A conscience is the ability to determine what is right from wrong and what ethical behavior is. A conscience is a learned trait. We mainly learn it from our parents and other people we grew up with, and to a certain extent, from schools, peers, and life's learning experiences as we grow up.

People with very little conscience or those with no conscience at all are referred to as criminal psychopaths or sociopaths. These people are able to steal, embezzle other people's money, or even kill without feeling guilty or contrite. They do not feel sorry for what they have done. Nor do they reflect on what they would do or have done, whether they hurt other people's feelings or generally caused hurt or damage to another person's life. If they feel regretful, it is only because they were caught. These are the kind of people who can lie while looking you straight in the eye. Their behavior is usually of the same pattern every single time regardless who they are dealing with.

Chronic, pathological, or sociopathic liars are another category. They may feel sorry for their actions, yet continue to deceive, twist the truth, or sugarcoat facts. Whatever the reason, these individuals have been accustomed to exhibit this undesirable behavior because they have always gotten away with it, a behavior which escalated in magnitude as they got older. Unfortunately, they sometimes no longer remember what the real facts are as they actually believe in their own lies.

On the other hand, while there are people who have no or little conscience, it is also possible for people to have too much of it. There are persons who are overburdened with an excessive amount of guilt. As a matter of fact, if we would look at our history, back in the early 1900s people were very much governed by a harsh and repressive type of conscience. Almost every action back then had a corresponding sin, making people fearful of many things they did.

But we have gone a long way as far as this era is concerned. Today, modern society shows us through movies, TV shows, and advertising materials what has drastically changed. Although most of the changes have been for good, we have obviously gone too far to the extreme. A movie actor once said in a line, "The crimes of today clearly reflect the society that we live in." How true!

Years ago, it was inconceivable to think of pre-med or law students cheating on their board exams and bar exams. But now, we watch the news with our jaws dropped as scandals on cheating on tests are publicized. Years ago, justice was swift and judges only took a short time to make a reasonable verdict. But now, we hear of judges being paid to make their decisions in favor of who paid how much. And those who are still of integrity have too many cases to review as they diligently study them one by one.

What better example of enigma in ethics and morality could we cite but that of politics and show business? Every day, when we watch the news, there is an issue on political and show business scandals. In politics, these are the people who are supposed to come from the most ethical of professions. Most of them are lawyers who are supposed to uphold the law. In show business, they call themselves professionals yet engage in ridiculous scandals. They are supposedly role models yet what do they do?

There is something terribly wrong in our society when we say to our children that the people who are supposed to lead, demonstrate, and act as our role models have failed us big time.

What I am trying to imply is that even if we have raised our children by applying the different methods of discipline we have chosen, we are still considered failures as a parent if

TEACHING OUR CHILDREN ETHICS AND MORALITY

we were not able to <u>imbue a sense of what is ethical, what is right or wrong, and the values we want them to acquire.</u>

<u>We have to bear in mind that we carry the responsibility to teach our children a sense of ethics and values, whether we are Catholic, Baptist, Christian, atheist, or Jew.</u> What they become as adults is dependent on how morally and ethically upright we have taught them to be. In my classes as a professor in the academy, I always emphasize moral ascendancy. In layman's terms, it means leading by example and credibility. The very same trait of what makes a good leader.

The best way to teach children ethics and morality is by being an ethical and moral example to them. What is the use of teaching them all of this if I myself cannot be emulated by my very own children? How can I be in a position of authority discussing money matters if I poorly manage my own funds? It would likewise be a mockery if we talk to our children about relationships and they see their parents having one relationship after another, having children out of wedlock, and not getting married at all afterward, and so on and so forth. Some may defend that they talk to their children about how not to be like them. I say, that is just so wrong. Parents are placed in their position to be role models and examples that children can emulate. If our excuse for preaching but not leading by example is such, then outright we have already removed ourselves as figures of authority (see chapter on Parental Authority).

When we teach ethics and morality, we always begin with a simple proposition. Anything you do that hurts other people and yourself is wrong. For my younger children, I put it this way: Do not do unto others what you don't want them to do unto you. Say, for example, we tell our children that it is bad to steal. They should understand that stealing is bad not just because you say so. We should let them learn that stealing is bad because it could hurt the feelings of the person you stole the item from or the item might have been for something important. Or in larger scales, we are not supposed to possess items that we did not rightfully earn. Or, we go to jail.

Just like when we explain to our children why it is bad to cheat in an examination, we tell them it is wrong not just because we say so but because it is unfair to the other students who studied and unfair to yourself because you deprive yourself the opportunity to gain knowledge by studying.

We have to live by this proposition in order to be able to teach this to our children. It is extremely difficult to teach our children the ethics and morality we ourselves do not believe and practice.

In reference to our proposition, we must also include that it is good to do loving things for other people and ourselves. With this additional proposition, we include the idea that loving other people and coming to their aid when needed is also a good thing. So many times we hear of other people witnessing a crime or a simple situation wherein someone is being mugged or someone's hand bag has been snatched. And what do witnesses do? They just stare. No one even bothers to call the police nor are there any gallant knights who would run after the person to catch the thief. (Again, the ability to discern of course must be exercised. We wouldn't want our children running every call that police officers are supposed to do.) This proposition should begin while the children are younger, like when they see another child being bullied or teased.

> ***"It is easier to build stronger children than repair broken men..." – Frederick Douglass***

There are two important things I have learned about ethics and morality. First, we need to be aware that when children become adolescents, they will challenge the values we have taught them in actual practice. They will challenge this verbally and vocally either by criticizing or scoffing at them.

The other thing I have learned is that it is absolutely normal for adolescents to challenge the ethics and morality we have taught them. And that it is not usual for them not to. If they do not, then something must be wrong. It is only in challenging what we teach them that individuals learn. And sometimes, it is the hard way.

Ethics and morality, if I may stress, are subjective. What is right for me may not be right for you. We must always remember to teach children that whatever they are taught, whether it is good or bad, it may be different for other people. And how do they resolve this? By telling them that no matter how different the perspective or point of view of another person is, it should be respected as long as it is not harmful to you or to another person.

14

THE ART OF NEGATIVE THINKING AND DESENSITIZATION

All of the chapters we have gone through tell us what to do if our children misbehave or show undesirable behavior. But what do we do when they appear to be the normal child that they are? Running around with their friends, playing dolls and computer games, following their bathing schedules, and eating their vegetables. Sad to say, some parents, because of their own personal hang-ups and frustrations, end up insisting that there must be something wrong with their child.

I remember a time when I was invited to talk to some

THE ART OF NEGATIVE THINKING AND DESENSITIZATION

parents in an elementary school. During the question-and-answer portion, one of the parents, teary-eyed, said, "My problem is my son. He wants to run for class president every year. But then he always ends up being the vice president or the class secretary or some other position." She said she felt frustrated that her son might be aiming too high for something he could not achieve.

I asked her if her son was expressing the same frustration. She said no. So I said, "There you go!" The problem is not with the child but with the parent. Parents are supposed to be happy that their child manifests at an early age his eagerness to achieve certain goals and takes the necessary steps to achieve them. What is wrong with that? In some cases, it seems like the parents are expecting too little of their children rather than aiming for something higher or better for them. I later on learned that the mother had her own hang-ups when she was the same age as her son. She also frequently ran for class officer but never landed a position. So there you go, a simple explanation.

So many times our negative past and thoughts make up who we are today. These negative thoughts are inside of us killing us softly. Our job is to help our children reach their goals by guiding them on how to reach their full potential.

Most books would tell us to overcome our fears or phobias through positive thinking. I have learned to deal with it the other way around. Let me tell you the advice I gave to that mother who complained about her son's ambitions. I told her to look at her son before she goes to bed every night while the boy is sleeping. And while looking at her son, I told her to whisper to herself her thoughts about her son's goals and ambitions that he, at a very young age, is aiming to achieve. So every night, she went to her son's room and uttered softly to herself these words: "What on earth are you thinking? Wanting to be class president? You will never become one! You're not as good as you think! Stop studying so hard because you'll never land a good job anyway when you grow up!" She did this for some time until she came to me and told me that she realized these were the very words her mother told her when she was younger. And although she had already grown up, these silent recordings continued to haunt her, and she was unconsciously passing them on to her child. In time, she came to a point of realization. She told me, "My son is an achiever; he has every right to pursue his goals. I know he will make it good someday. It was so foolish of me to think that way about him." I refer to this as a process of desensitization. This is the same process I teach my children when they express fear of something.

I recall an instance when my son came into our room in the middle of the night to sleep beside me. This became his habit for almost a week. He appeared to be very frightened. After a moment of query, we learned that he was having nightmares that a huge bear was attacking him. This fear, he acquired after watching a suspense thriller on television.

My solution? To desensitize him by letting him watch the reruns over and over again. Absurd as most people may think it was, I went on with the "program." And so, he watched it probably more than five times. Either with me or with his other siblings or with his nanny. By the fifth time, he told me it was only a puppet and that the production crew didn't even do a good job with the other effects.

This strategy also proved to be effective when I advised my youngest daughter, only five at that time, to make it a habit to raise her hand in every subject of her class at least once a day. It didn't matter that her answers were wrong. What mattered for me was that she overcame her fear of talking in front of a lot of people.

But as in other techniques we have mentioned in this book, negative thinking is not for everyone, and there are many factors to be considered before using it as a strategy to modify behavior.

When parents or guardians find certain aspects of their children to be annoying, whether it is a cause of their own hang-ups or not, it is recommended that we first determine what is "normal" behavior for a child in their developmental stage. If the child's behavior is then confirmed to not be normal as expected, then we need to use the various discipline strategies as needed to change the child's behavior to a more satisfactory level. But if his behavior is what could normally be expected from a child of their age, then you need to change your attitude as a parent.

If negative thinking is used to deal with negative feelings toward either natural or stepchildren and you find that it does not considerably change your feelings, then you may need the help of a professional for counselling, either for yourself and the child or even for the whole family, in order to improve family feelings or interaction.

Negative thinking is not just one of the discipline strategies that we can use to modify undesirable behavior. It is also a powerful tool that you may find helpful in conquering your own fears and personality problems.

15

STEPPARENTING AND THE BLENDED FAMILY
(Source: helpguide.org)

When families "blend" to create stepfamilies, things rarely progress smoothly. Some children may resist changes, while parents can become frustrated when the new family doesn't function like their previous family. While changes to family structure require adjustment time for everyone involved, these guidelines can help blended families work out their growing pains and live together successfully.

BOND with your new family. No different from establishing rapport as mentioned earlier in this book. As a stepparent, focus more on developing positive relationships with your stepchildren. You will become more successful when you focus more on what the children need. Age, gender, and personality may not be relevant in some cases since children or people in general have a basic need and want that should be met as an antecedent to a great relationship.

The first step is to plan. You and your partner have decided to make a life together and form a new blended family that includes children from one or both of your previous relationships. Congratulations. What lies ahead can be both a rewarding and a challenging experience. It can take a long time for a blended family to begin to feel comfortable and function well together.

While you as parents are likely to approach remarriage and a new blended family with great joy and expectation, your kids or your new spouse's kids may not be nearly as excited. They'll likely feel uncertain about the upcoming changes and how they will affect relationships with their natural parents. They'll also be worried about living with new stepsiblings, whom they may not know well, or worse, ones they may not even like. To give yourself the best chance of success, it's important to start planning how a blended family will function before the marriage even takes place.

Laying the foundations for a blended family

Having survived a painful divorce or separation and then finding a new loving relationship, the temptation can often be to rush into remarriage and a blended family without first laying solid foundations. By taking your time, you give everyone a chance to get used to each other, and used to the idea of marriage.

Too many changes at once can unsettle children. Blended families have the highest success rate if the couple waits two years or more after a divorce to remarry, instead of piling one drastic family change onto another.

Don't expect to fall in love with your partner's children overnight. Get to know them. Love and affection take time to develop.

Find ways to experience "real life" together. Taking both sets of kids to a theme park every time you get together is a lot of fun, but it isn't reflective of everyday life. Try to get the kids used to your partner and his or her children in daily life situations.

Make parenting changes before you marry. Agree with your new partner on how you intend to parent together, and then make any necessary adjustments to your parenting styles *before* you remarry. It'll make for a smoother transition and your kids won't become angry at your new spouse for initiating changes.

Don't allow ultimatums. Your kids or new partner may put you in a situation where you feel you have to choose between them. Remind them that you want *both* sets of people in your life.

Insist on respect. You can't insist people like each other but you can insist that they treat one another with respect.

Limit your expectations. You may give a lot of time, energy, love, and affection to your new partner's kids that will not be returned immediately. Think of it as making small investments that may one day yield a lot of interest.

Given the right support, kids should gradually adjust to the prospect of marriage and being part of a new family. It is your job to communicate openly, meet their needs for security, and give them plenty of time to make a successful transition.

Bonding with your new blended family

Early in the formation of a blended family, you as a stepparent may want to focus on developing positive relationships with your stepchildren. You will increase the chances of success by thinking about what the children need. Age, gender, and personality are not irrelevant, but *all* children have some basic needs and wants that should be met as a precursor to a great relationship.

Children want to feel:

- **Safe and secure.** Children want to be able to count on parents and stepparents. Children of divorce have already felt the upset of having people they trust let them down, and may not be eager to give second chances to a new stepparent.
- **Loved.** Kids like to see and feel your affection, although it should be a gradual process.
- **Seen and valued.** Kids often feel unimportant or

invisible when it comes to decision making in the new blended family. Recognize their role in the family when you make decisions.
- **Heard and emotionally connected.** Creating an honest and open environment free of judgment will help kids feel heard and emotionally connected to a new stepparent. Show them that you can view the situation from their perspective.
- **Appreciated and encouraged.** Children of all ages respond to praise and encouragement and like to feel appreciated for their contributions.
- **Limits and boundaries.** Children may not think they need limits, but a lack of boundaries sends a signal that the child is unworthy of the parents' time, care, and attention. As a new stepparent, you shouldn't step in as the enforcer at first, but work with your spouse to set limits.

Let the child set the pace.

Every child is different and will show you how slow or fast to go as you get to know them. Some kids may be more open and willing to engage. Shy, introverted children may require you to slow down and give them more time to warm up to you. Given enough time, patience, and interest, most children will eventually give you a chance.

How children adjust to blended families

Kids of different ages and genders will adjust differently to a blended family. The physical and emotional needs of a two-year-old girl are different than those of a thirteen-year-old boy, but don't mistake differences in development and age for differences in fundamental needs. Just because a teenager may take a long time accepting your love and affection doesn't mean that he doesn't want it. You will need to adjust your approach with different age levels and genders, but your goal of establishing a trusting relationship is the same.

Young children under 10		May adjust more easily because they thrive on cohesive family relationships. Are more accepting of a new adult. Feel competitive for their parent's attention. Have more daily needs to be met.
Adolescents age 10-14		May have the most difficult time adjusting to a stepfamily. Need more time to bond before accepting a new person as a disciplinarian. May not demonstrate their feelings openly, but may be as sensitive, or more sensitive, than young children when it comes to needing love, support, discipline, and attention.
Teenagers 15 or older		May have less involvement in stepfamily life. Prefer to separate from the family as they form their own identities. Also may not be open in their expression of affection or sensitivity, but still want to feel important, loved, and secure.

Gender Differences – general tendencies:

Both boys and girls in stepfamilies tend to prefer verbal affection, such as praise or compliments, rather than physical closeness, like hugs and kisses.

Girls tend to be uncomfortable with physical displays of affection from their stepfather. Boys seem to accept a stepfather more quickly than girls.

> Family isn't whose blood you carry
> It's who you love and who loves you back

16
RIGHTS OF THE CHILD – SUMMARY
A Summary of the Rights Under the Convention on the Rights of the Child
(United Nations)

Article 1 (Definition of the child): The Convention defines a 'child' as a person below the age of 18, unless the laws of a particular country set the legal age for adulthood younger. The Committee on the Rights of the Child, the monitoring body for the Convention, has encouraged States to review the age of majority if it is set below 18 and to increase the level of protection for all children under 18.

Article 2 (Non-discrimination): The Convention applies to all children, whatever their race, religion or abilities; whatever they think or say, whatever type of family they come from. It doesn't matter where children live, what language they speak, what their parents do, whether they are boys or girls, what their culture is, whether they have a disability or whether they are rich or poor. No child should be treated unfairly on any basis.

Article 3 (Best interests of the child): The best interests of children must be the primary concern in making decisions that may affect them. All adults should do what is best for children. When adults make decisions, they should think about how their decisions will affect children. This particularly applies to budget, policy and law makers.

Article 4 (Protection of rights): Governments have a responsibility to take all available measures to make sure children's rights are respected, protected and fulfilled. When countries ratify the Convention, they agree to review their laws relating to children. This involves assessing their social services, legal, health and educational systems, as well as levels of funding for these services. Governments are then obliged to take all necessary steps to ensure that the minimum standards set by the Convention in these areas are being met. They must help families protect children's rights and create an environment where they can grow and reach their potential. In some instances, this may involve changing existing laws or creating new ones. Such legislative changes are not imposed, but come about through the same process by which any law is created or reformed within a country. Article 41 of the Convention points out that when a country already has higher legal standards than those seen in the Convention, the higher standards always prevail.

Article 5 (Parental guidance): Governments should respect the rights and responsibilities of families to direct and guide their children so that, as they grow, they learn to use their rights properly. Helping children to understand their rights does not mean pushing them to make choices with consequences that they are too young to handle. Article 5 encourages parents to deal with rights issues "in a manner consistent with the evolving capacities of the child." The Convention does not take responsibility for children away from their parents and give more authority to governments. It does place on governments the responsibility to protect and assist families in fulfilling their essential role as nurturers of children.

Article 6 (Survival and development): Children have the right to live. Governments should ensure that children survive and develop healthily.

Article 7 (Registration, name, nationality, care): All children have the right to a legally registered name, officially recognized by the government. Children have the right to a nationality (to belong to a country). Children also have the right to know and, as far as possible, to be cared for by their parents.

RIGHTS OF THE CHILD – SUMMARY

Article 8 (Preservation of identity): Children have the right to an identity – an official record of who they are. Governments should respect children's right to a name, a nationality and family ties.

Article 9 (Separation from parents): Children have the right to live with their parent(s), unless it is bad for them. Children whose parents do not live together have the right to stay in contact with both parents, unless this might hurt the child.

Article 10 (Family reunification): Families whose members live in different countries should be allowed to move between those countries so that parents and children can stay in contact, or get back together as a family.

Article 11 (Kidnapping): Governments should take steps to stop children being taken out of their own country illegally. This article is particularly concerned with parental abductions. The Convention's Optional Protocol on the sale of children, child prostitution and child pornography has a provision that concerns abduction for financial gain.

Article 12 (Respect for the views of the child): When adults are making decisions that affect children, children have the right to say what they think should happen and have their opinions taken into account. This does not mean that children can now tell their parents what to do. This Convention encourages adults to listen to the opinions of children and involve them in decision-making – not give children authority over adults. Article 12 does not interfere with parents' right and responsibility to express their views on matters affecting their children. Moreover, the Convention recognizes that the level of a child's participation in decisions must be appropriate to the child's level of maturity. Children's ability to form and express their opinions develops with age and most adults will naturally give the views of teenager's greater weight than those of a preschooler, whether in family, legal or administrative decisions. Article 12 (Respect for the views of the child): When adults are making decisions that affect children, children have the right to say what they think should happen and have their opinions taken into account.

Article 13 (Freedom of expression): Children have the right to get and share information, as long as the information is not damaging to them or others. In exercising the right to freedom of expression, children have the responsibility to also respect the rights, freedoms and reputations of others. The freedom of expression includes the right to share information in any way they choose, including by talking, drawing or writing.

Article 14 (Freedom of thought, conscience and religion): Children have the right to think and believe what they want and to practice their religion, as long as they are not stopping other people from enjoying their rights. Parents should help guide their children in these matters. The Convention respects the rights and duties of parents in providing religious and moral guidance to their children. Religious groups around the world have expressed support for the Convention, which indicates that it in no way prevents parents from bringing their children up within a religious tradition. At the same time, the Convention recognizes that as children mature and are able to form their own views, some may question certain religious practices or cultural traditions. The Convention supports children's right to examine their beliefs, but it also states that their right to express their beliefs implies respect for the rights and freedoms of others.

Article 15 (Freedom of association): Children have the right to meet together and to join groups and organizations, as long as it does not stop other people from enjoying their rights. In exercising their rights, children have the responsibility to respect the rights, freedoms and reputations of others.

Article 16 (Right to privacy): Children have a right to privacy. The law should protect them from attacks against their way of life, their good name, their families and their homes.

Article 17 (Access to information; mass media): Children have the right to get information that is important to their health and well-being. Governments should encourage mass media – radio, television, newspapers and Internet content sources – to provide information that children can understand and to not promote materials that could harm children. Mass media should particularly be encouraged to supply information in languages that minority and indigenous children can understand. Children should also have access to children's books.

Article 18 (Parental responsibilities; state assistance): Both parents share responsibility for bringing up their children, and should always consider what is best for each child. Governments must respect the responsibility of parents for providing appropriate guidance to their children – the Convention does not take responsibility for children away from their parents and give more authority to governments. It places a responsibility on governments to provide support services to parents, especially if both parents work outside the home.

Article 19 (Protection from all forms of violence): Children have the right to be protected from being hurt and mistreated, physically or mentally. Governments should ensure that children are properly cared for and protect them from violence, abuse and neglect by their parents, or anyone else who looks after them. In terms of discipline, the Convention does not specify what forms of punishment parents should use. However any form of discipline involving violence is unacceptable. There are ways to discipline children that are effective in helping children learn about family and social expectations for their behavior – ones that are non-violent, are appropriate to the child's level of development and take the best interests of the child into consideration. In most countries, laws already define what sorts of punishments are considered excessive or abusive. It is up to each government to review these laws in light of the Convention.

Article 20 (Children deprived of family environment):

RIGHTS OF THE CHILD – SUMMARY

Children who cannot be looked after by their own family have a right to special care and must be looked after properly, by people who respect their ethnic group, religion, culture and language.

Article 21 (Adoption): Children have the right to care and protection if they are adopted or in foster care. The first concern must be what is best for them. The same rules should apply whether they are adopted in the country where they were born, or if they are taken to live in another country.

Article 22 (Refugee children): Children have the right to special protection and help if they are refugees (if they have been forced to leave their home and live in another country), as well as all the rights in this Convention.

Article 23 (Children with disabilities): Children who have any kind of disability have the right to special care and support, as well as all the rights in the Convention, so that they can live full and independent lives.

Article 24 (Health and health services): Children have the right to good quality health care – the best health care possible – to safe drinking water, nutritious food, a clean and safe environment, and information to help them stay healthy. Rich countries should help poorer countries achieve this.

Article 25 (Review of treatment in care): Children who are looked after by their local authorities, rather than their parents, have the right to have these living arrangements looked at regularly to see if they are the most appropriate. Their care and treatment should always be based on "the best interests of the child." (See Guiding Principles, Article 3)

Article 26 (Social security): Children – either through their guardians or directly – have the right to help from the government if they are poor or in need.

Article 27 (Adequate standard of living): Children have the right to a standard of living that is good enough to meet their physical and mental needs. Governments should help families and guardians who cannot afford to provide this, particularly with regard to food, clothing and housing.

Article 28: (Right to education): All children have the right to a primary education, which should be free. Wealthy countries should help poorer countries achieve this right. Discipline in schools should respect children's dignity. For children to benefit from education, schools must be run in an orderly way – without the use of violence. Any form of school discipline should take into account the child's human dignity. Therefore, governments must ensure that school administrators review their discipline policies and eliminate any discipline practices involving physical or mental violence, abuse or neglect. The Convention places a high value on education. Young people should be encouraged to reach the highest level of education of which they are capable.

Article 29 (Goals of education): Children's education should develop each child's personality, talents and abilities to the fullest. It should encourage children to respect others, human rights and their own and other cultures. It should also help them learn to live peacefully, protect the environment and respect other people. Children have a particular responsibility to respect the rights of their parents, and education should aim to develop respect for the values and culture of their parents. The Convention does not address such issues as school uniforms, dress codes, the singing of the national anthem or prayer in schools. It is up to governments and school officials in each country to determine whether, in the context of their society and existing laws, such matters infringe upon other rights protected by the Convention.

Article 30 (Children of minorities/indigenous groups): Minority or indigenous children have the right to learn about and practice their own culture, language and religion. The right to practice one's own culture, language and religion applies to everyone; the Convention here highlights this right in instances where the practices are not shared by the majority of people in the country.

Article 31 (Leisure, play and culture): Children have the right to relax and play, and to join in a wide range of cultural, artistic and other recreational activities.

Article 32 (Child labour): The government should protect children from work that is dangerous or might harm their health or their education. While the Convention protects children from harmful and exploitative work, there is nothing in it that prohibits parents from expecting their children to help out at home in ways that are safe and appropriate to their age. If children help out in a family farm or business, the tasks they do should be safe and suited to their level of development and comply with national labour laws. Children's work should not jeopardize any of their other rights, including the right to education, or the right to relaxation and play.

Article 33 (Drug abuse): Governments should use all means possible to protect children from the use of harmful drugs and from being used in the drug trade.

Article 34 (Sexual exploitation): Governments should protect children from all forms of sexual exploitation and abuse. This provision in the Convention is augmented by the Optional Protocol on the sale of children, child prostitution and child pornography.

Article 35 (Abduction, sale and trafficking): The government should take all measures possible to make sure that children are not abducted, sold or trafficked. This provision in the Convention is augmented by the Optional Protocol on the sale of children, child prostitution and child pornography.

Article 36 (Other forms of exploitation): Children should be protected from any activity that takes advantage of them or could harm their welfare and development.

Article 37 (Detention and punishment): No one is allowed to punish children in a cruel or harmful way. Children who break the law should not be treated cruelly. They should not be put in prison with adults, should be able to keep in contact with their families, and should not be sentenced to death or life imprisonment without possibility of release.

Article 38 (War and armed conflicts): Governments must do everything they can to protect and care for children affected by war. Children under 15 should not be forced or recruited to take part in a war or join the armed forces. The Convention's Optional Protocol on the involvement of children in armed conflict further develops this right, raising the age for direct participation in armed conflict to 18 and establishing a ban on compulsory recruitment for children under 18.

Article 39 (Rehabilitation of child victims): Children who have been neglected, abused or exploited should receive special help to physically and psychologically recover and reintegrate into society. Particular attention should be paid to restoring the health, self-respect and dignity of the child.

Article 40 (Juvenile justice): Children who are accused of breaking the law have the right to legal help and fair treatment in a justice system that respects their rights. Governments are required to set a minimum age below which children cannot be held criminally responsible and to provide minimum guarantees for the fairness and quick resolution of judicial or alternative proceedings.

Article 41 (Respect for superior national standards): If the laws of a country provide better protection of children's rights than the articles in this Convention, those laws should apply.

Article 42 (Knowledge of rights): Governments should make the Convention known to adults and children. Adults should help children learn about their rights, too. (See also article 4.)

Articles 43-54 (implementation measures): These articles discuss how governments and international organizations like UNICEF should work to ensure children are protected in their rights.

17
THE RIGHTS OF THE PARENTS

Modern psychology has taught us the importance of effective parenting skills in raising our children to become well-rounded adults.

Time and again, we ask ourselves as parents whether we are raising our children well enough to be good and acceptable persons. We constantly ask ourselves if the path of guidance we gave them was the right one. Because of this overly conscious thought, we end up being slaves to our children, and we forget that we, too, have rights and lives of our own to live. We constantly involve ourselves with their activities

– supervising, planning, and helping them run their daily lives.

It is unfortunate to find parents in this situation, but most of us at some point are guilty of this. Most would even claim that their children are their lives. Not that there's anything wrong with that. In my earlier chapters, I mentioned that our children are transients in our lives. If we make them our lives, then what will become of us when it is time for them to move out on their own and discover and deal with the world by themselves?

Whenever a parent gives up their rights and freedom in order to cater to their child's whims, reality is, they feel taken advantage of at the end of the day – even though they have done this to themselves. And because of these feelings, they rebound and end up unconsciously being angry with the child, making them less effective as a parent.

The earlier chapter clearly enumerated the rights of the child—their rights as a person and rights from the government they dwell in. But I also believe that parents are entitled to rights and feelings and that it is an absolute mistake to ignore or neglect them.

Allow me to enumerate Dr. Fitzhugh Dodson's rights as follows:

1. **The right to your own feelings and the right to express them.** We emphasize in our earlier chapters to allow our children to express negative and positive feelings accordingly. As a parent, you have the

THE RIGHTS OF THE PARENTS

same rights as they do. Feel free to express these feelings not just because it would emotionally do you good but because it presents the children the reality that parents have feelings too, which should also be respected. Like any other human being, parents can also feel anger and resentment, and they have a whole lot of ways to express happiness.

2. **The right to be the authority in your own home.** I know parents who complain about their teenager's long periods of time on the telephone, coming home late, and constantly asking for additional allowance, but they don't do anything about it. Others allow their children to play loud, banging music that could shatter your eardrums. The most they do is complain, yet they do not reprimand their children. Tolerating a child's unpleasant and rude behavior is not good for parents or children. As I would always tell my own teenage daughter, "For as long as you live in our house, you live by our rules."

3. **In the hierarchy of family loyalties and priorities, you have the right to have your marriage come first and the relationship with the children come second.** As studies have observed, many families are now child-centered rather than marriage-centered. I once saw a sign in a bookstore that said: "The greatest gift a father can give his children is to love their mother." I totally agree. Once a marriage maintains its own independent center of gravity, the children definitely benefit from a happy and stable marriage.

4. **The right to take periodic vacations as a parent.** Every year, employees are entitled to vacation leave from work. Many people also take regular vacations from their jobs on a weekly basis. But what about the job of being a parent? Aren't parents entitled to vacations from this difficult and time-consuming job? This is unrealistic and unhealthy.

   Even employees who are not able to make use of their yearly vacations feel stale from their jobs. And mind you, they are paid workers. How much more do we suffer from our job as a parent? That is why it is advisable for a mother or father or both parents to every so often leave the children to their grandparents or nannies and take off for the weekend. During this time, they do not have to play the role of mother or father or guardian but instead enjoy themselves as husband and wife or lover or single parent. Even a night out at the movies will do.

5. **You have the right to make mistakes in bringing up your children.** Can you just imagine how life would be if all we ever worried about was how we are as parents? But what can we expect when we are all unprepared for this job? I have yet to meet someone who tells me that they are absolutely prepared to parent. And even if we are all prepared with master's and doctorate degrees on child psychology, we will still find ourselves making on-the-job mistakes with our very own children. I can tell you that from my own experience with my children.

THE RIGHTS OF THE PARENTS

6. **The right to pursue your own career and interests.** We may be parents—a mother, a father—but first and foremost, we are persons with interests and needs to fulfil. As I have mentioned, it is psychologically unhealthy to allow our lives to revolve around our children, while we neglect our responsibility to ourselves to fulfil our own needs and aspirations and develop our talents.

7. **The right to be irrational.** There are times when children are irrational. Teenagers are emphatically irrational; politicians, movie stars, and even judges are sometimes irrational. So why should parents be the only human beings on earth who should be rational all the time? Let me cite an example: Sometimes, when my children constantly ask me why I do or decide what I do, I simply tell them, "Because I say so" or "Because I just want to and you have to respect that. I know it's irrational and it might make me feel uncomfortable later on that I acted that way, but don't copy it unless you will take responsibility the way I do." And that's that. It is normal for all of us to have irrational feelings from time to time. Make allowances for it and stop thinking that parents have no right to feel this way.

8. **The right to be infallible, imperfect human beings.** This means we have the right to have bad days, to be cross, illogical, biased, dogmatic, and opinionated at times. We also have the right to be furious at our children at times, to feel like pampering

ourselves at times, and to be uptight at times. Remember: we are human. We are not and cannot be perfect.

9. **The right to preserve your sanity.** Any parent who stays at home with their kids all day, especially those with preschoolers, has the right to spend time alone without their children to preserve their parental sanity. Or just plain sanity, period. The constant company of children, especially young children, can wear on an adult physically and psychologically. There are numerous ways to find time alone for yourself. You can hire a baby sitter, leave your children with their grandparents for a while, or if your youngster is three, you can send them to a day care so that they are away from you for a few hours. Something. Not that you do this every single day. And of course I need not remind you that ability to discern and common sense are of utmost importance whichever way you decide to do it. You can go on a vacation with your husband or by yourself. However you do it, you have every right to protect yourself from feeling trapped with your children. You have the right to preserve your sanity by spending time alone without your children.

10. **The right to be yourself.** We have stressed in this book that every child is unique. Each child is a combination of chromosomes that no one can duplicate on this planet. And that person has the right to be the person they want and choose to be.

THE RIGHTS OF THE PARENTS

That applies to you as a parent. You are free to read books and attend workshops and seminars on parenting. Whatever it is, choose what your heart desires. At the end of the day, it is you who should decide how you will parent. These books, venues, and materials are there to guide you, but the decision is yours and yours alone.

18
DEVELOPMENTAL STAGES

INFANCY

A child is considered an infant from birth until they begin to crawl or walk (this may vary from one child to another), which covers approximately the first year of their life. In infancy, the child forms the most fundamental attitude towards himself and his world. The developmental task of infancy is <u>*learning the basic trust of himself and his world, or it's opposite*</u>. When a baby is not ignored when he cries, is fed properly when hungry, gets a lot of hugs and kisses, he will develop a good sense of himself and his world and would have an optimistic viewpoint towards life. Most parents don't usually have problems with their child at this stage. As a matter of fact, most parents do a very good job with their children during the infancy stage, and discipline problems do not usually arise at this time. Nonetheless, child-raising problems during infancy are important most particularly to first time parents. The means by which parents handle these problems will be indicative whether it will strengthen or weaken the discipline process that will begin at a later stage.

There are two things that we need to remember during this stage: *First*, the importance of rapport as the foundation of discipline. Rapport is what makes us much-loved in the eyes of our child, and rapport is what makes them want to obey us. *Second*, we all know that there are children that are easy to raise than others. And because each child embodies a different combination of genes, each child has a unique temperament that shows at birth. According to a study conducted by researchers on babies, the first week of life of babies already show differences among them in terms of temperamental factors. Their rate of crying, intensity of reactions, distractibility, approach and withdrawal in response to a stimulus, degree of persistence in the face of obstacles are characteristics that makes one child different from another.

TODDLERHOOD

Toddlerhood begins when the baby first learn to crawl and walk and lasts approximately until his second birthday. Toddlerhood is the age of exploration. They are little scientists who will explore almost everything that arouses their curiosity.

Your child's developmental task at this stage is to _either learn self-confidence or self-doubt_. A child in this stage should be given the opportunity to explore and research her environment. She should be able to use her motor and cognitive skills – to run, to walk, jump, hide, play house, play race car, play doctor-nurse, try new sounds, and socialize with friends and relatives. If they are allowed and encouraged to do these activities, this kind of environment will allow them to acquire self-confidence which will be an integral part of their self-concept throughout their life.

However, if your toddler grew up to an alien and purely adult environment, surrounded by what seemed to be a thousand no's and restrictions, then, they are bound to develop self-doubt. They would then grow up to become repressed individuals.

For toddlers to develop self-confidence, the formula is very simple. Childproof your house (read: Environment Control) to reduce the no-no's and maximize their opportunity to explore their surroundings.

FIRST ADOLESCENCE

From the second to the third birthday, a child is in his first adolescence stage. In preschool educational circles, it is referred to as the terrible twos. I actually find this an unfair title for these little tots. It simply labels the typical behavior of this age as being obnoxious without giving a parent a real insight into what is going on psychologically within the child at this stage in his life.

This stage is labeled instead as first adolescence. This stage

DEVELOPMENTAL STAGES

is clearly similar to the teenage years which we may even call second adolescence. Both stages are transitional stages. Teenage is a transition from childhood to adulthood. While first adolescence is a transition from babyhood to childhood. During these stages, children exhibit forward movements toward independence coupled with backward movements toward dependence upon their parents. This is usually a confusing stage for parents because it is sometimes difficult to determine, especially for teenagers if they want independence or dependence at specific situations. In both stages, the development of a negative self-concept precedes the development of a positive self-concept. This means that your two year old will first begin to develop his self-concept by resisting everything you tell him to do. At this stage, they tend to become negativistic, and would often say "No!" or do exactly what you ask them not to do.

This is the stage where children do the extreme. It is difficult for them at this stage to do simple, clear-cut choices and stick to it. Their feelings will shuttle back and forth with contrary feelings until the parent feels they are about to lose their patience. It is also at this stage where the child's ability to share, wait and take his turn is very limited. This stage definitely takes a huge demand on the parent's patience.

And because of a child's annoying behavior at this time in their lives, it is very important for parents to understand the positive aspect of this developmental phase. Much as the behavior of a teenager is annoying to parents (I am sure those like myself who have and had teenagers could relate), I eventually came to accept that beyond that annoying surface is a youngster trying to find their self-identity. Just like a two-year-old child, he is trying to do exactly the same thing. A two-year-old's negativism and rebelliousness is actually an indication of positive growth. Without these changes, he would remain in the equilibrium of babyhood. We wouldn't want that, do we? As adults, we know in life that transitional changes in our life go through certain processes. And sometimes, these procedural processes are not easy to go through.

And in spite of this negativism, your two-year-old child can be charming, exuberant and innocent with his view of an unspoiled world.

Sometimes, I find it so ironic that parents desire their child to grow up to become adults with strong and dynamic personalities. But then have trouble accepting these personalities when their child is a two-year-old. But what is the major quality of a first adolescent? Nothing but dynamic! How could we miss his energetic enjoyment for life, his need for instant gratification, his protests against restraint, and enthusiastic commitment to the world that he experiences? This dynamic quality of your child is a very important psychological resource. Instead of repressing this inevitable stage in your child's life, it is important to foster and channel its force properly.

Learning self-identity versus social conformity is the task of this developmental stage, a miniature version of the same developmental task your child will experience much later in his teenage years. And in order for them to be able to define who or what they want to their own satisfaction, they have to go through a stage of negating and defying what their parents want them to do.

Without knowing the psychological characteristics of this stage of development, it would be very difficult to discipline a child of this age. They could either end up making too many demands for control or may become afraid to exercise control, constantly giving in to the excessive demands of the child, thereby producing the Spoiled Brat Syndrome.

The discipline needed at this stage calls for a firm hand at the parental wheel, but at the same time, considerable flexibility in rules and regulations. Absolute and rigid rules are not advisable at this stage of development because the child is full of ambivalent feelings and urges.

PRESCHOOL PERIOD

The preschool period extends from the third to the sixth birthday of the child. Although three, four, and five-year-olds are different in many ways; they are grouped together in one stage because of the nine developmental tasks during these years. The mastery of these tasks will determine their personality structure by the time they are six years old.

The developmental tasks at this stage are:

1. To fulfill his biological needs for both large and small muscle development

2. To develop a control system for his impulses
3. To separate himself from his mother
4. To learn the give and take of relationships among his peers
5. To express or repress his feelings
6. To stabilize his gender identity as male or female
7. To form his basic attitude towards sexuality
8. To work his way through the resolution of his relationships in his family
9. To go through a period of development that is responsive to intellectual stimulation.

Some of these developmental tasks appear in partial form in earlier stages, but it is in this stage that they play a major part in your child's life. At this stage, your child has now entered into an equilibrium where he is now a delight to be around. This stage has also proven to be the best age to start the discipline strategies discussed in the earlier chapters of this book. At the age of four, the child may pose some discipline problems such as defiance and negativism, but the fifth year usually goes smoothly as another year of equilibrium begins.

MIDDLE CHILDHOOD

From the sixth to the eleventh birthday of your child, his

preschool stage brings about a stable integration of his personality. Middle childhood usually covers a long time span than the earlier stages. It is also believed to be a tranquil period in your child's life. His developmental task at this time is to _learn mastery versus inadequacy_.

His self-identity at this stage is based on how well he masters the specific skills and accomplishments that are demanded in school, his peer groups, and at home. A good self-identity is based on your child's confidence to be able to do the things that are required and demanded of him. If he is not able to master specific tasks at hand, his sense of adequacy and inferiority is affected.

This is a point in your child's life where he wants to feel a sense of belonging within his family and a sense of freedom from them at the same time.

PREADOLESCENCE

In our previous chapter, we stated that our child's personality is reasonably stable during middle childhood (ages six through ten). But we must keep in mind that as our children grow, this is accompanied by different stages in their development, or they shall never grow up psychologically to become an adult.

If the other stages of development had positive tasks, this is the first stage in which the task is to disorganize. Although this is not permanent disorganization in your child's personality, this is the kind that makes room for the new gathering of psychological patterns that constitute adulthood. It is the same concept as breaking down an old building in order to put up a new and improved one. In relation to his personality, childhood patterns are broken up to make way for a higher organization. The first break up process occurs during preadolescence. This "tearing down" process usually begins around their eleventh birthday – the age when preadolescence starts, and lasts approximately up to their thirteenth birthday.

Believe me when I say it is going to be easy to determine when your child has reached this stage. They suddenly become obnoxious in every way you can think of. I remember when my daughter, Paulina, made me realize that she had already reached this stage. I would usually let her assist her younger siblings to perform tasks such as cleaning up their closets, fixing their beds, to supervising them while they do their homework. Although I am around while these tasks are being performed, my objective was to give her a sense of responsibility as the eldest child. To look after the younger ones. However, during this particular time when I asked her to help her sister clean up her closet, she blurted out loudly: "WHY CAN'T SOME PEOPLE HERE BE RESPONSIBLE ENOUGH TO CLEAN UP THEIR OWN MESS? WHAT AM I HERE, A MAID? I FIND IT SO UNFAIR THAT SOME PEOPLE IN THIS FAMILY THINK THAT MY ONLY ROLE IS TO ASSIST EVERYONE WITH WHAT THEY ARE SUPPOSED TO DO!" and she goes on and on, tackling issues from her privacy (she shares her room with her sister) to chores in the house.

This kind of behavior is extremely difficult for us parents but we must realize that it is important and necessary for our child to behave this way. We must come to accept that no matter how uncomfortable this process is for us, every preadolescent needs the chance to let out some untamed behavior in one form or another. Not that they do it on purpose, but because they are at the stage where they need to tear down their building of childhood personality and build up a new one that would eventually turn them into the adults that they will become. Remember: the preadolescent who never had difficult dealings with adults, has defied adult rules, or has gotten into trouble are usually the ones that have a great deal of difficulty making it successfully through adolescence into adulthood.

At this stage, no matter what discipline problems you have with your child might as well be accepted as a fact that preadolescence is generally a rough stage for parents to go through.

EARLY ADOLESCENCE

Although adolescence does not really have a fixed time boundary, we can logically define adolescence as the stage of development between puberty and adulthood. Puberty usually takes place between twelve and thirteen years old while adulthood begins on his twenty-first birthday. Now, to make an arbitrary division, we may say that early adolescence encompasses the ages thirteen to fifteen, while late adolescence spans from sixteen to twenty-one.

Early and late adolescence share the same developmental task: _to form an ego identity that is different from that of their parents_. During early adolescence, our teenager tries to answer the question: "Who am I?" Your child seeks to answer this question within the framework of his family, although with considerable upheaval. In late adolescence, he also grapples with that question within the larger framework of society. Here, he copes with real questions on occupational choice and sexual maturity.

An adolescent may be perceived to be confusing at times since a part of them wants to become emotionally independent of his parents and stand on his own feet, while the other part of him wants to remain a dependent child, with all the comfort and security associated with being emotionally dependent on their parents. Your child will fluctuate back and forth between wanting to be dependent and independent.

Early adolescence begins with puberty. This is the time wherein our child needs to cope with a totally new phenomenon within themselves: sexual urges. Not only does he need to adjust to these new and powerful impulses, but he must also adjust to a new body which is totally different from what he was accustomed to: the girls begin their menstruation, breasts start to develop, curves become visible, while boys start to grow more hair on their upper lips and underarms as well as significant changes in their voice.

Our children at this stage start to overcome the emotional attachment they have with their parents and achieve emotional independence. And what more convenient way to

DEVELOPMENTAL STAGES

break away from your parents but to revolt and find flaws in them. And by becoming hostile, it becomes easier for the adolescent to cut the emotional cords of his childhood and launch out as the person he wants to be.

The main mistake most of us parents make is to take this phase personally. We tend to believe that if we handle things right, our teenager will not revolt against us. But realistically, we have no choice. The only choice we have is whether our child would have a normal or abnormal rebellion. By abnormal rebellion, we refer to trouble with the law, drug abuse, or sexual difficulty. In some cases, parents unfortunately turn their child's rebellion into an abnormal one by the way they handle the situation. Therefore, our task at this stage is to learn to expect and how to deal with this reality, rather than focus on the stress and heartaches this stage will cause us. Studies on the development of this stage have emphasized that the relationship with your child during this phase would have an unsettled nature. This is generally normal. If I were to look back during my own adolescent years, I would remember how frustrated my parents were towards me. But that stage came to pass. In this case, the stage must come to pass. We need not take issues too seriously and personally. Although it is easier said than done, I too found difficulty during this stage in my daughter's life. I said to myself: What have I done to deserve this? Why does she do the things she knows we would strongly object to? And as much as the drama came to pass, so did the obnoxious behavior.

Now, let me stress that based on research and my personal experience, most of the strategies we talked about would work fine up to approximately the age of twelve. But when our youngster becomes a teenager, we will wonder why these strategies cease to work. Although some of the strategies will continue to work throughout your child's teen years, this is precisely because they are based on a relationship between equals rather than a relationship between the adult parent and the young child. The methods that will prove to be workable at this point would be the maintenance of emotional building of rapport, the feedback technique, the mutual-problem solving technique, the family council, and contracting.

LATE ADOLESCENCE

Late adolescence occupies the years between sixteen and twenty-one. Your teenager will realize that they have overcome the issue of independence and that they are already half adults.

As we have mentioned in early adolescence, your child aims to answer the question "Who am I?" within the framework of his family. While in late adolescence, they aim to establish their ego identity within the larger framework of the society. Their task at this stage becomes more complex because (1) _they need to decide and prepare for a vocation_ – what do they want to become when they grow up into a full pledged adult now not only needs a concrete answer but steps on how to achieve it. (2) _To work out a satisfactory relationship with the_

DEVELOPMENTAL STAGES

<u>opposite sex and establish stable patterns of a love life</u> – again, I emphasize that at this stage, they aim to conform to social norms. Sexual preferences become clearer to them at this stage. (3) *<u>Complete his liberty from parents and family</u>*.

Late adolescence is usually a difficult time for parents to handle because it also coincides with their own developmental stage in life. Most of us would then be in our middle ages. So when the late adolescent and the middle aged come together, expect a clash of the titans.

In most of my researches, psychologists and psychiatrists have mentally categorized late adolescence to span from sixteen to twenty-one. Although at the age of eighteen, they are legally considered adults, they are still in an emotional battle with themselves whether to be dependent or independent, then, they are still considered adolescents.

Apart from my own, I have raised children of this age including my twin brothers who lived with me at separate periods when they were ten and seventeen, I stood in for my parents to be their legal guardian. Although my youngest brother may be classified as a parent's ideal child, it was probably because he understood the difficulties we were going through as a physically divided family. There was almost no indication of rebellion during this stage of development in his life. Contrary to his twin brother who also stayed with me for only five years with whom I had an extremely difficult period.

I say this to emphasize once more that our children are

individuals with different characteristics. They have innate traits we must understand and learn to deal with. Looking back, perhaps the reason why I had difficulty handling my other brother was because I too was going through a difficult period in my life at that time. My twin brothers are now family men and I couldn't be any prouder to see that they turned out to be loving and responsible individuals. The age when they no longer rebel - either openly or subtly.

So to end my book, I would like to stress that parenting should be a joy for many people. It disheartens me most of the time when I see that parents are more harassed than joyful when they engage in activities with their children, like going to the park, picnic on the beach, or strolling at the mall. Believe me when I say that there is no sight more pleasing than to see a parent enjoying moments with their children no matter how simple it is.

I hope that in advocating children's rights and promoting the joys of parenting, this book would help other parents to change the usual situations we have with our children during the years they have been entrusted to us. The premise of this book is very simple. Our role is to give our children roots and wings. Roots to know where home is and wings to fly away and exercise what is taught them.

Being a parent has been one of the most rewarding aspects of my life. Beyond titles and other achievements. I am sure most of you would agree that this is also as important in your life as it is in mine.

About the Author:

Marikit Villasis-Corbin is mother to Paulina, Jethro, Stephanie, and Akihiro Hermès and loving wife to Ken Corbin. A lifestyle and fashion blogger, an advocate of children, and an animal rights proponent, she has practiced and rendered her services to both the government and private sector as a forensic child psychologist.

She considers herself fortunate to have worked with elite agencies such as the FBI and Interpol by conducting interviews and assessment in child abuse cases as both an expert witness and a forensic specialist.

She is now CEO of Empress Consulting LLC, a human resource training and development firm that focuses on life skills and capacity building training to integrate successfully into modern society or contribute in a meaningful way to the community. She practices child development and psychology independently.

Marikit's life mission is to bring out the best in every individual who accepts her in their life path and to inspire others to be the best they can be as they pay the good deed forward.

CPSIA information can be obtained
at www.ICGtesting.com
Printed in the USA
FSOW03n0006131016
26073FS